{} human rights *first*

The Asylum Filing Deadline

Denying Protection to the Persecuted and Undermining Governmental Efficiency

September 2010

Table of Contents

About Human Rights First

Human Rights First believes that building respect for human rights and the rule of law will help ensure the dignity to which every individual is entitled and will stem tyranny, extremism, intolerance, and violence.

Human Rights First protects people at risk: refugees who flee persecution, victims of crimes against humanity or other mass human rights violations, victims of discrimination, those whose rights are eroded in the name of national security, and human rights advocates who are targeted for defending the rights of others. These groups are often the first victims of societal instability and breakdown; their treatment is a harbinger of wider-scale repression. Human Rights First works to prevent violations against these groups and to seek justice and accountability for violations against them.

Human Rights First is practical and effective. We advocate for change at the highest levels of national and international policymaking. We seek justice through the courts. We raise awareness and understanding through the media. We build coalitions among those with divergent views. And we mobilize people to act.

Human Rights First is a non-profit, non-partisan international human rights organization based in New York and Washington D.C. To maintain our independence, we accept no government funding.

Acknowledgments

The principal authors of this report were Eleanor Acer, Tori Andrea, Lori Adams and Asa Piyaka. Ms. Andrea, a Georgetown Fellow at Human Rights First, was the primary researcher. Research was also conducted by Asa Piyaka, a former Kroll Human Rights Fellow, Lori Adams and Annie Sovcik. Additional research, writing and/or editing was contributed by Annie Sovcik, Anwen Hughes, Reena Arya, Tad Stahnke, Isabel Toolan, Ruthie Epstein and Alexandra Wisotsky. Human Rights First wishes to express its appreciation for the legal and factual research conducted by Jayne Fleming and other pro bono attorneys at the law firm of Reed Smith LLP. Wendy Crandall typeset the report.

We wish to thank the many refugees and asylum seekers, pro bono attorneys, legal representation organizations, faith-based and community groups, legal experts, former government officials and adjudicators, U.S. Citizenship and Immigration Services and others who provided information that was included in, or helped to inform, this report.

Human Rights First gratefully acknowledges the support provided for our pro bono legal representation project by, among others, the Fund for New Jersey and the Fund for New Citizens of the New York Community Trust.

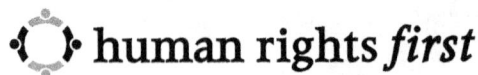

◖◗ human rights *first*

Headquarters	Washington D.C. Office
333 Seventh Avenue	100 Maryland Avenue, NE
13th Floor	Suite 500
New York, NY 10001-5108	Washington, DC 20002-5625
Tel.: 212.845.5200	Tel: 202.547.5692
Fax: 212.845.5299	Fax: 202.543.5999

www.humanrightsfirst.org

I. Executive Summary

The filing deadline on U.S. asylum requests, enacted as part of a 1996 immigration law, should be eliminated. As Human Rights First's research confirms, this technical filing requirement is barring legitimate refugees with well-founded fears of persecution from receiving asylum in the United States and is leading to the unnecessary expenditure of government resources. The deadline pushes the cases of credible refugees into the overburdened immigration courts, diverts limited time and resources that could be more efficiently allocated to assessing the actual merits of asylum applications, and is not needed to counter abuse in the system.

In 1996, Congress passed, and President Clinton signed into law, a provision barring an individual from seeking asylum if he or she did not apply for protection within a year of arriving in the United States. In the 12 years since the deadline began barring asylum requests,[1] more than 53,400 applicants have had their requests for asylum denied, rejected or delayed due to the filing deadline. Despite the fact that there are exceptions, this filing deadline has barred from asylum refugees who have suffered persecution or have well-founded fears of persecution in their home countries. These refugees have included victims of political, religious, ethnic, and other forms of persecution from Burma, China, Colombia, Guinea, Iran, and Sierra Leone.

Through its research and *pro bono* legal representation of asylum seekers in the United States, Human Rights First has learned of many genuine refugees who have had their asylum requests rejected, denied or significantly delayed due to the filing deadline and its application by U.S. adjudicators. For example, as detailed in this report:

- An Eritrean woman, who was tortured and sexually assaulted due to her Christian religion, was denied asylum in the United States based on the filing deadline even though an immigration judge found her testimony credible and compelling.

- A student who was jailed by the Burmese military regime for his pro-democracy activities was denied asylum by the United States based on the filing deadline despite his isolation in the U.S. and lack of English.

- A Chinese woman who feared persecution and torture in China for her assistance to North Korean refugees was determined by the immigration judge to face a clear probability of torture but was denied asylum based on the filing deadline and ordered removed by the U.S. Board of Immigration Appeals.

- A man from Togo who was tortured because of his pro-democracy activities had his asylum request rejected based on the filing deadline, and the request was only granted - three years after his initial filing - after subsequent immigration court litigation.

- A gay man who was attacked, tortured and faced a clear probability of persecution in Peru had his asylum request rejected based on the filing deadline.

- A Congolese nurse who was persecuted and tortured due to her human rights advocacy and her Catholic faith was denied asylum based on the filing deadline even though the immigration court found her to be a credible refugee who faced a clear probability of persecution.

- A teenager who was battered, kidnapped, and raped in Albania while plans were made to traffic her into prostitution was denied asylum after her application was ruled untimely.

The United States has long led the international community in protecting refugees who have fled from political, religious and other forms of persecution. But because of the filing deadline, the United States is denying protection to refugees in ways that are inconsistent with this county's leadership in, and commitment to, protecting refugees in accordance with the 1951 Convention Relating to the Status of Refugees and its 1967 Protocol.

Many refugees are unable to file within a year of their arrival: they may arrive in this country traumatized from persecution, unable to speak English and without any knowledge of the U.S. asylum system. Some do not know that they might be eligible for asylum. Many do not have the resources to retain legal counsel, and *pro bono* resources are scarce or simply not available in many parts of the country. In a recent study conducted by Human Rights First, we found that 17 percent of the new *pro bono* clients we took on for legal representation with their asylum claims had not, prior to acceptance into our program, filed for asylum within a year of their arrival, despite the fact that they were refugees in need of protection.

Not only are legitimate refugees denied asylum based on the filing deadline, but the deadline also undermines the protection of refugees in other ways, including by:

- Returning some refugees to persecution and leaving others with only temporary forms of protection in the U.S. that put them at risk of deportation, detention, and prolonged instability; and

- Dividing refugee families, leaving young children stranded in difficult and dangerous circumstances abroad and separated from their refugee parents in the United States who have not been provided with the immigration status (of asylum) that would allow them to petition to bring their children and spouses to safety in the U.S.

The filing deadline also undermines the efficiency of the asylum and immigration court adjudication systems. The overwhelming majority of the over 53,400 cases rejected based on the filing deadline at the U.S. asylum office have been referred into the immigration court removal

system. As detailed in this report, the filing deadline and its application by U.S. adjudicators has led the United States to:

- Push the cases of genuine refugees – estimated to number over 18,000 - into the over-burdened immigration court system instead of resolving them more efficiently at the initial asylum office level;

- Delay the adjudication of asylum cases that were referred into the backlogged immigration court system but could have otherwise been granted asylum more promptly before the asylum office;

- Divert time and resources at both the asylum office level and the immigration courts, expending limited government resources litigating a technicality, when those resources could instead be allocated to evaluating the actual merits of asylum cases, or could simply be saved or re-allocated to other matters; and

- Undercut governmental interests in integration by depriving genuine refugees of the ability to become permanent residents and U.S. citizens while also making it more difficult for them to access jobs and education.

The exceptions to the filing deadline – for changed or extraordinary circumstances – have not prevented genuine refugees from being denied asylum in the United States. Indeed, as detailed in this report, many refugees with well-founded fears of persecution have been denied asylum by U.S. adjudicators despite the fact that there are exceptions to the filing deadline. The lack of federal court review on the issue in most circuits also means that refugees in many parts of the country cannot get mistaken filing deadline denials corrected by the federal courts.

While proponents of the filing deadline were, at the time it was created, concerned about the abuse of the asylum system by individuals filing fraudulent claims, this procedural impediment has actually prevented refugees with *credible* non-fraudulent asylum cases from receiving asylum in the United States. Moreover, as detailed in this report, U.S. immigration authorities implemented a series of major reforms to the asylum system beginning in 1995. These reforms targeted incentives for filing fraudulent applications, increased staffing at the asylum office, and improved the pace of adjudications so that individuals who did not have credible cases were put into the deportation process much more quickly. In the intervening years, additional controls to counter abuse have also been added to the system. As detailed in this report, there are numerous mechanisms in place that are actually designed to combat abuse and fraud, including:

■ Asylum applications must be signed under penalty of perjury by both the asylum applicant and the individual preparing the application to ensure appropriate consequences for false statements;

■ Any fraudulent asylum applicants are permanently barred from receiving any immigration benefit, meaning that they would never be able to work legally in the United States or receive lawful permanent resident status here;

■ Each asylum seeker's identity must be checked in a series of Department of Homeland Security and other federal databases - these checks can help identify fraudulent cases as well as any individual who might present a security risk;

■ Asylum officers and immigration judges are not authorized to grant asylum until the applicant's fingerprints have been run through the FBI fingerprint database, and asylum applicants' names are also checked against the FBI name database;

■ U.S. Citizenship and Immigration Services has an Office of Fraud Detection and National Security that aids in identifying fraudulent asylum claims; and

■ Documents provided in support of asylum claims are often sent to the Department of Homeland Security's Forensic Document Laboratory where

technicians analyze the documents' authenticity and, compare them to the lab's library of foreign travel and identity documents.

And, of course, individuals who file fraudulent claims - as well as preparers and attorneys - can be investigated and criminally prosecuted.

When the filing deadline was enacted as part of the Illegal Immigration Reform and Immigrant Responsibility Act of 1996 (IIRIRA), then President Clinton said that he would "seek to correct provisions in this bill that are inconsistent with international principles of refugee protection, including the imposition of rigid deadlines for asylum applications." The former Immigration and Naturalization Service (INS) had stressed that the imposition of a filing deadline was a response to a problem that had already been addressed through its reforms - reforms that U.S. immigration authorities subsequently reported had successfully addressed abuse in the asylum system.

At the time the law was enacted, several key Congressional supporters of the deadline made clear that it was not intended to bar legitimate applicants and that they were committed to revisiting the filing deadline if it did not provide adequate protection for these asylum seekers. The deadline has not provided this protection, and has instead prevented genuine refugees from receiving asylum, while also causing counterproductive inefficiencies in the adjudication system. It is time to revisit - and eliminate - the filing deadline. By removing this procedural impediment, Congress would improve the effectiveness of the asylum adjudication system and reaffirm this country's commitment to protecting those who seek refuge from persecution.

Introduction

"And she's still a beacon, still a magnet for all who must have freedom, for all the pilgrims from all the lost places who are hurtling through the darkness, toward home."
- President Ronald Reagan speaking of the United States as the "shining city" in his Farewell Address to the Nation in January 1989

"Through the Refugee Act and continued humanitarian aid, America's leadership in international relief efforts and in defense of human rights has helped expand protections for countless refugees, internally displaced persons and other victims around the world."
- President Barack Obama, marking World Refugee Day in June 2010[2]

The United States has a long history of protecting those who flee from political, religious and other forms of persecution, and has long been a leading voice for the protection of refugees around the world. In the wake of World War II, the United States helped lead efforts to create an international refugee protection regime to ensure that the world's nations would never again refuse to extend shelter to refugees fleeing persecution and harm.[3] The United States has committed to comply with the central guarantees of the 1951 Refugee Convention and its 1967 Protocol (the "Refugee Convention" and "Protocol," respectively).[4] Thirty years ago, the United States passed the Refugee Act of 1980 in order to bring the country's laws into compliance with its commitments under these treaties, by incorporating into U.S. law the Convention's definition of a "refugee" and the principle of non-refoulement, which prohibits the return of refugees to persecution.[5]

The United States also leads the global community in its commitment to providing refuge and humanitarian assistance to refugees. In 2009, nearly 12,000 refugees were granted asylum by the U.S. Citizenship and Immigration Services asylum office, and over 10,000 more were granted asylum by U.S. immigration courts.[6] In addition to providing protection to asylum seekers who have already reached its shores, the United States has also played a leading role in the resettlement of refugees who are stranded in refugee camps and other difficult or dangerous situations abroad. In fact, this country has brought more than 2.4 million refugees to safety here in

the last thirty years, and the U.S. resettlement program has served as a model to the rest of the world.[7] The United States is also a primary supporter of the United Nations refugee agency, the UN High Commissioner for Refugees (UNHCR).[8]

Though the United States has historically been a leader in protecting victims of persecution, several provisions that limit access to asylum were enacted into law as part of the Illegal Immigration Reform and Immigrant Responsibility Act (IIRIRA) in 1996. One of these provisions, known as the "one-year filing deadline," bars an individual from receiving asylum – even if that individual has a well founded fear of persecution – if his or her application is not filed within one year of arrival in the United States.

In cases where an asylum seeker has not applied within one year of arrival, or is determined not to have established that he or she applied within one year of arrival, the asylum seeker may be able to secure an exemption from the one-year bar if he or she can demonstrate either "changed circumstances which materially affect the applicant's eligibility for asylum or extraordinary circumstances relating to the delay in filing,"[9] and can establish that he or she filed within a reasonable time given the exception. Congress intended these exceptions "to provide adequate protections to those with legitimate claims of asylum."[10] However, as detailed in Section IV of this report, these exceptions have not prevented genuine refugees from being denied asylum.

At the time the deadline was debated in Congress, and during the years since, a wide range of government officials and experts have expressed concern about the impact of the deadline on legitimate asylum seekers.[11] Medical and legal experts have explained that legitimate asylum seekers often arrive in the United States with few resources, unable to speak English, and without relatives, extended family, and community connections. Their initial efforts in the United States are focused on addressing basic needs, like housing and food, and tracking down family here or abroad. These challenges are multiplied for those refugees who are also caring for small children or other relatives.[12] In addition, many asylum seekers have experienced severe physical and psychological trauma in their home countries, making the adjustment even more difficult.[13]

These linguistic, medical, and other challenges can pose significant obstacles to filing for asylum within the first year of arrival for many refugees. Refugees who have experienced the most severe trauma are often the ones left most vulnerable by the filing deadline.[14] In fact, in a study conducted prior to the enactment of the filing deadline, Human Rights First (then Lawyers Committee for Human Rights) found that in a random sampling of 200 of its pro bono refugee clients, only 37 percent had applied for asylum within one year of arrival.[15]

In the years since the deadline was enacted, Human Rights First has witnessed the significant effects of this technical requirement on both refugees and the adjudication system. In 2009, we began conducting research to document the impact of the deadline on asylum seekers and refugees, including our own *pro bono* asylum clients, as well as on the asylum office and immigration court systems. This research included requests for, and reviews of, relevant governmental statistics and other information; interviews with attorneys, refugees, and other experts; research into various procedures; and a review and analysis of Human Rights First's own *pro bono* asylum cases, as detailed in the Appendix to this report. This report reflects our findings and recommendations.

I. Refugees Denied Asylum and Protection From Return to Persecution

"[I]f the time limit and its exceptions do not provide adequate protections to those with legitimate claims of asylum, I will remain committed to revisiting this issue in a later Congress."

- Senator Orrin Hatch, September 27, 1996

The filing deadline is a procedural hurdle that can lead refugees – who by definition have suffered persecution or have well-founded fears of persecution if returned to their countries – from being granted protection in the United States. In the course of our research, Human Rights First identified numerous cases of refugees who were determined by adjudicators to have well-founded fears of persecution – some of whom were determined to face an even greater clear probability of persecution if returned home - but had their asylum claims rejected, denied or delayed based solely on the filing deadline. For example:

- **A Burmese student who was jailed by the Burmese military regime for his pro-democracy activities was denied asylum by the United States based on the filing deadline.** [16] The student fled to the United States after being jailed for several years for his pro-democracy activities. The student did not speak English, lived in isolation after his arrival, and did not learn about asylum until several years later after he met other Burmese refugees. The U.S. immigration court concluded that he did not file for asylum within a reasonable time. The student was denied asylum even though he was found to be credible and to face a clear probability of persecution, requiring the withholding of his removal. The Board of Immigration Appeals and the U.S. Court of Appeals for the Sixth Circuit did not overturn the decision to deny him asylum based on the filing deadline.

- **An evangelical Christian from Uzbekistan who faced a clear probability of religious persecution was denied asylum based on the filing deadline.** [17]

He had come to the United States to study and later became fearful to return after learning that there had been a significant increase in persecution against evangelical Christians in Uzbekistan. The increase in attacks, beatings and detention of evangelical Christians was reported by the U.S. Department of State and by the U.S. Commission on International Religious Freedom. The young man was advised by an attorney that he was not eligible for asylum because he had been in the United States more than one year – even though the significant increase in religious persecution should have made him eligible for an exception to the filing deadline based on changed circumstances. The young man eventually hired a new attorney, and submitted an asylum application. Ultimately, the immigration court acknowledged that it was more likely than not that the young man would be persecuted in Uzbekistan for being an Evangelical Christian and granted him withholding of removal. However, both the immigration court and the Board of Immigration Appeals denied asylum because of the filing deadline.

- **A political activist from Pakistan who was arrested and tortured for putting up political posters was found to face a clear probability of persecution if returned to Pakistan but was denied asylum based on the filing deadline.** He had been attacked and beaten unconscious by members of a rival political party in Pakistan, and was later arrested and tortured by government authorities after putting up political posters. [18] The immigration court ruled that he was credible and faced a clear probability of persecution in Pakistan but found him ineligible for asylum based on the filing deadline. The immigration court granted him withholding of removal, which requires a higher burden of proof than asylum but has no filing deadline. The Board of Immigration Appeals affirmed the decision.

In fact, this report is full of examples of refugees whose cases were denied asylum even though U.S. adjudicators concluded that they had credible and well-founded fears of persecution – and in some cases faced a clear probability of persecution if returned home. These refugees came from a wide range of countries where human rights advocates, pro-democracy activists and religious, ethnic and other minorities face severe persecution.

Each year, thousands of applicants struggle to overcome the one-year filing deadline. Some of these individuals are ultimately granted asylum, often after lengthy litigation; some receive withholding of removal, a limited form of protection; others are denied asylum and are ordered returned to persecution in their home countries. Many of these cases require more time and resources in our immigration system than they would if the filing deadline were not an issue. The inefficiencies caused by the filing deadline are discussed in detail in Section II of this report.

According to U.S. government statistics, between 1998 and 2009:

- Over **100,411** asylum seekers – which constitute **27 percent** of those filing asylum applications with U.S. Citizenship and Immigration Services – were identified as having filing deadline issues.[19]

- Of these, over **53,400** asylum seekers – which comprise **15 percent** of the total number of asylum seekers, and **53 percent** of the late-filing applicants – had their requests for asylum rejected by the U.S. asylum office based on the filing deadline.[20] The overwhelming majority of these cases were then referred into the immigration courts.

- Neither the U.S. immigration courts nor the Board of Immigration Appeals (BIA) report or even track the number of asylum cases denied at those levels based on the filing deadline.[21]

- A review of four months of BIA decisions revealed that about **19 percent** of those cases were appealed to the BIA level in part because of the filing deadline.[22]

Human Rights First routinely takes on, for *pro bono* legal representation, cases of asylum seekers who have been in the United States for over one year before applying for asylum. We accept these (and other) cases only after conducting in-depth interviews which last several hours, and then conducting assessments to determine whether we believe each individual is actually a "refugee" who has suffered past persecution or has a well-founded fear of persecution.

In a new study conducted in conjunction with this report, Human Rights First found that even with the filing deadline in place, 20 percent of the asylum clients we took on for pro bono representation from 2005 through 2008 had not filed timely. Further, more than half of Human Rights First's successful asylum seekers with filing deadline issues had taken more than two years to submit their applications, and one-third of these refugees took more than four years to apply for asylum.[23]

During the years 2005 through 2008, 20 percent of Human Rights First's new *pro bono* refugee cases had filing deadline issues, meaning in most cases that, at the time we took their cases on, their asylum requests had already been rejected by the asylum office based on the filing deadline.[24] For example:

- **A political refugee from Cote d'Ivoire was denied asylum even though an immigration court concluded that he faced a clear probability of persecution.** The refugee, a former official in Cote d'Ivoire, was in the United States when the president he had served under was accused of fomenting a coup and was killed. [25] Government officials began targeting anyone politically affiliated with the former president. When they were unable to find the former official, the government forces kidnapped his children and arrested his wife. The former official applied for asylum in the United States, but despite changed circumstances in his country, his asylum claim was rejected at the asylum office because he did not file within one year of entering the United States. The immigration court granted him only withholding of removal in light of the filing deadline, a form of relief which recognizes that the asylum seeker is more likely than not to face persecution if returned to his home country. However, because withholding is a temporary form of protection, he was not able to bring his wife and children to safety in the United States.

- **A Chinese student who practices Falun Gong was denied asylum because of the filing deadline.** This asylum seeker began practicing Falun Gong while he was a university student in China, although he had to practice in secret because he knew that the Chinese government sought to stop the practice and was involved in a campaign of brutal repression against practitioners.[26] After coming to the United States to continue his studies, he became a representative for a Falun Gong group at his university. Through this role he became more well-known for his practice of Falun Gong and he fears that the Chinese authorities would detain or persecute him if he returns to China now. He learned about asylum a few years after his arrival in the United States and filed an application for asylum without the assistance of an attorney. The asylum office rejected his claim based on the filing deadline. He then met with a representative from Human Rights First which provided him with *pro*

bono counsel for his immigration court hearing. Due to delays in the immigration courts, his next hearing will not be until mid-2011, nearly four years after he filed his asylum application.

- **A nurse from Zimbabwe who was persecuted due to her peaceful political protest and labor rights advocacy had her asylum request rejected due to the filing deadline.** [27] The nurse was involved with her local union and a peaceful opposition political party. As a result of these affiliations and her humanitarian efforts to procure supplies and assistance for a state-run hospital, she was attacked and called a traitor. Fearful because of these attacks and continued harassment of her and her family, she applied for asylum in the United States. Unfortunately, her original attorney failed to file her asylum application in time to meet her one year filing deadline. The nurse's asylum request was rejected at the asylum office based on the filing deadline, and her case was referred into immigration court proceedings. She then spoke to attorneys at Human Rights First, and they assigned her *pro bono* attorneys to represent her in court. The nurse was ultimately granted withholding of removal, though she was not granted asylum.

In some cases, the immigration judge will decide that a refugee who is barred from asylum due to the filing deadline can have his or her deportation to the country of feared persecution withheld. In other cases, refugees who have well-founded fears of persecution but cannot meet the higher standard under U.S. law for withholding of removal are ordered deported back to their countries of persecution based on the one-year bar. While the differing standards have a long history under U.S. law, this anomaly can lead the United States to deport back to persecution refugees with well-founded fears of persecution—including in cases implicating the asylum filing deadline.

applicants with well-founded fears of political, religious, or other forms of persecution. For example:

- **A Chinese woman who feared torture and persecution due to her assistance to North Korean refugees was denied asylum based on filing deadline and ordered by the Board of Immigration Appeals to return to China.** The woman, who was a member of a human rights group, fled from China to the United States after learning that the Chinese police were looking for her because she provided food and shelter to North Korean refugees.[32] She later applied for asylum defensively after being put into immigration court removal proceedings. In support of her request for protection, she submitted affidavits from two other members of her human rights organization who attested to the torture they suffered when being interrogated by Chinese officials about their human rights activities. She also submitted an affidavit from a U.S. citizen detained for two years by Chinese authorities who testified to the torture suffered by prisoners who were detained in China for aiding North Korean refugees. The U.S. immigration court held that the woman's asylum claim was time-barred as it was not filed within one year of her arrival in the United States. Though the immigration court determined that she faced a clear probability of torture in China, granting her withholding of removal, she was denied asylum. The BIA affirmed the denial of asylum, reversed the court's grant of withholding, and ordered that the woman be removed to China. The U.S. Court of Appeals for the Third Circuit later reversed that decision and reinstated the withholding grant, finding that it was more than likely that she would be tortured if returned to China.

- **A woman from Senegal who fled forced marriage and FGM was denied asylum due to filing deadline and ordered deported.** The woman is a member of the Djola ethnic group, which practices female genital mutilation ("FGM"), and was informed that she had to undergo FGM and enter an arranged marriage with a man 40 years her senior.[33]

Withholding of removal

Withholding of removal is a limited form of protection that is only available to an applicant who can prove that it is "more likely than not" that he or she would be subject to persecution if returned to his or her home country.[28] This steep "clear probability of persecution" standard is higher than the well-founded fear of persecution standard for establishing eligibility for asylum.[29]

But refugees who are granted only withholding of removal are often left in very difficult situations. Not only are they at risk of detention in the United States or deportation to other countries, but they cannot bring their spouses and minor children to join them in the United States as derivative asylees. As a result, these refugee families can remain permanently separated, leaving refugee children in dangerous situations abroad without the protection of their parent. In addition, the ability of these refugees to integrate into the community in the United States is further undermined because, unlike asylees, they are not allowed to file for lawful permanent resident status, which would provide them more stability in the United States and allow them to later apply for U.S. citizenship.[30] These challenges are detailed in Section II of this report.

In a number of cases, U.S. adjudicators have noted that while the asylum seekers' fears of persecution might not meet the high withholding of removal standard, they may indeed meet the reasonable fear standard for asylum, but they must still be denied asylum due to the filing deadline.[31] Asylum seekers who are barred by the filing deadline, and are not found to meet the high standard for withholding of removal, are thus ordered back to their home countries – even if they are indeed credible

She refused and went to the police for protection, but the police declined to intervene. The woman ultimately fled to the United States. She did not apply for asylum for several years, explaining later that she believed that the practice would change in her country with the passage of criminal laws prohibiting FGM. When she learned that her sister was forced to undergo FGM, despite the new laws, she realized that she was still in danger of being subjected to the practice if she returned to Senegal. She then applied for asylum, four years after her arrival in the United States. The immigration court found the woman to be "genuinely credible" and found that her claim was consistent with country conditions. But she was denied asylum based on the filing deadline. In considering her eligibility for withholding, the judge noted that there might indeed be a "reasonable possibility" that she would be subjected to FGM on return, but concluded that she did not meet the higher "more likely than not" standard for withholding of removal.[34] The BIA agreed. The U.S. Court of Appeals for the Fourth Circuit, in declining to overturn the denial of withholding, also noted that "there is evidence in the record that tends to support [her] claim that if she returns to Senegal, she will face a risk of FGM,"[35] and the dissenting judge wrote that the woman "presents a mountain of evidence that clearly demonstrates that the likelihood of her being forced to undergo FGM is certainly 100%."[36] The woman even filed a petition asking the U.S. Supreme Court to review the decision, but the petition was not granted.

- **A woman from Colombia who feared political persecution from a militant group in Colombia was ordered deported after being denied asylum based on the filing deadline.** The woman sought asylum based on fears of persecution by the FARC (the Revolutionary Armed Forces of Colombia).[37] In her testimony, she described being targeted by the FARC because of her peaceful political activities and her assistance to the victims of the FARC. The woman donated goods from her bakery to rallies held by her political party; she also donated baked goods to help farmers who had been displaced by the FARC. She was threatened repeatedly by the FARC. The woman's son was killed, and FARC members threatened her further, specifically referring to her son's death. Although she moved to different locations in Colombia, the threats continued. The woman finally fled to the United States. Several years later she applied for asylum. The woman explained that she did not know about asylum, and that she did not have the money to consult with an attorney. The immigration court denied asylum based on the filing deadline, and the BIA upheld the filing deadline denial, stating that "[neither] lack of information nor lack of financial resources is an 'extraordinary circumstance'" that would excuse the delay in filing. The immigration court and the BIA acknowledged "her and her family's tragic experiences" but both also concluded that she did not meet the higher standard for withholding of removal. Consequently, she was provided no protection from being deported to Colombia.

- **An asylum seeker from Algeria who presented "grave" evidence concerning fears of persecution by terrorists in his home country was ordered removed.** The man testified that terrorists in Algeria treat former and current military conscripts as enemies and often set up fake checkpoints to kill them.[38] He also testified that two of his friends who were in the military had been killed by terrorists, as was his cousin. Despite his fears of persecution as a former military conscript, both the immigration court and the BIA denied his request for asylum based on the filing deadline. They also concluded that he did not meet the higher standard for withholding of removal. The U.S. Court of Appeals for the Seventh Circuit, which reviewed the denial of withholding of removal, stressed that "[t]he evidence in this case is grave" but did not overturn the decision denying all relief.[39] The asylum seeker was ordered deported to Algeria despite the grave risks.

While some of the asylum seekers profiled in this report should have been found eligible for an exception to the filing deadline, their cases were still rejected or denied asylum based on the filing deadline. As detailed in Section IV of this report, genuine refugees are often denied asylum based on the filing deadline despite the existence of exceptions to the filing deadline.

U.S. Commitments Under International Human Rights Standards

A filing deadline that prevents an asylum case from being adjudicated on its merits is inconsistent with U.S. leadership in protecting refugees. Article 33 of the Refugee Convention prohibits the return of refugees to persecution, and Article 34 calls on signatories to facilitate the assimilation and naturalization of refugees.[40] The UNHCR Executive Committee, of which the United States is a member, has specified that failure to comply with technical requirements such as filing deadlines "should not lead to an asylum request being excluded from consideration."[41] In fact, António Guterres, the UN High Commissioner for Refugees, speaking at a March 2010 event marking the 30th anniversary of the U.S. Refugee Act of 1980, described the filing deadline as "diverg[ing] from international standards" and said that it "makes it more difficult for many asylum seekers to establish their need for protection."[42]

Refugees Who File Timely Unable to Prove Date of Entry

The filing deadline also presents challenges even for those asylum seekers who do apply within a year of their arrival. First, as discussed in Section II of this report, assessing compliance with the filing deadline is a component of all asylum cases - even those in which applicants file on time. Second, the filing deadline often ends up being a significant impediment for a subset of timely filers, specifically legitimate refugees who do not have documentary proof of their date of arrival in the United States. The filing deadline requires applicants to prove timely filing by an exceedingly high "clear and convincing evidence" standard.[43] Applicants are often expected to prove two different dates: (1) the date the asylum application was filed, and (2) the date that the applicant arrived in the United States. Some adjudicators have denied asylum based on the filing deadline because the applicant did not have travel documents proving the exact date they entered the United States, which the adjudicators took to mean that the applicant could not prove compliance with the deadline.[44]

Thus, practically speaking, asylum seekers run afoul of the filing deadline either by actually failing to file within one year, or if they are considered unable to prove their exact date of arrival in the United States by "clear and convincing evidence." These claims are ruled untimely even if the asylum seeker is found to be credible and have a well-founded fear of persecution.

In a number of cases reviewed by Human Rights First, adjudicators denied asylum to applicants - even though the applicants presented testimonial or other evidence relating to their date of entry - because the adjudicators concluded that the applicants could not meet the "clear and convincing evidence" burden to prove timely filing. From these cases, it is clear that legitimate asylum seekers who have actually filed for asylum within one year of their arrival in the United States have had their cases rejected, denied or delayed because of the filing deadline.

- **A Congolese human rights advocate who escaped torture with the help of nuns was denied asylum based on the filing deadline because she could not prove the date she entered the United States.** The refugee was a nurse who was active in a human rights organization in the Democratic Republic of Congo (DRC).[45] Because of her human rights advocacy and her Catholic faith, the Congolese government falsely accused her of being involved with a rebel group. She was arrested by government officials and detained for three weeks. During that time, she was tortured and raped by prison guards after she denied any connection to the rebel group. The nurse was able to escape and traveled first to Mexico with the help of several nuns who had visited her in the prison. She then fled on to the United States, crossing over the southern border without being inspected by immigration officials. She applied for asylum affirmatively within her first year in the United States. Her request for asylum was denied by a U.S. immigration court which concluded that she could not prove the date she entered the United States. After three years of litigation, the nurse was finally extended only "withholding of removal" which does not provide the permanent protection of asylum.

- **An Ethiopian political activist and torture survivor was denied asylum based on the filing deadline despite providing proof of his date of entry.** The man was a member of an opposition political group and was detained for a year by the Ethiopian government because of his peaceful political activities.[46] During this detention, government officials frequently tortured him. When the man finally escaped, he fled first to Mexico, and then on to the United States, crossing the border. He filed for asylum within one year of entering the country, but had no proof of his date of entry because the documents relating to his travel to the United States were taken by smugglers. To prove compliance with the deadline, the man submitted an affidavit from his sister, with whom he had lived in the United States since he arrived. He also submitted an affidavit from a migration expert, confirming that smugglers typically take and do not return travel documents. Nonetheless, the man's asylum request was rejected on the basis that he did not establish that he had filed for asylum within one year of his entry. As a result of this denial of protection, and because he would have to wait many months for an

immigration court hearing, the man did not further pursue his request for protection in the United States and left the country for Canada.

- **A woman from Sierra Leone was initially denied asylum because she did not have a passport showing her date of entry.** This refugee escaped Sierra Leone after surviving a rebel attack in which her husband and son were killed in front of her, and she herself was brutally attacked.[47] Though she could not read or write English and had no money to pay for a lawyer, she filed for asylum in the United States within one month of her arrival with the help of some acquaintances. The asylum office rejected her application, stating that she could not prove that she had been in the United States for less than one year because she did not have a passport showing her date of entry. The woman did have another valid identification document, which was issued in Sierra Leone and proved that she must have entered the United States at some point after it was issued. With the help of *pro bono* attorneys arranged by Human Rights First, she made that argument to the immigration judge. More than a year after she initially filed her asylum application, the judge acknowledged that she had filed within one year of entry and granted her asylum.

II. Inefficient and Counterproductive – for the Government and the Country

"[A] deadline will gum up the process and have us spinning around an issue – when a person entered the country – which is difficult to prove, rather than just hearing the claim and getting to the substance."

- Director of INS Office of International Affairs, before the filing deadline became law[48]

In her home country of Eritrea, a refugee who we will call "Dehab" was taken from her home and forcibly conscripted into military service by the government.[49] While in a military training camp, she became an active member of a Christian church. Because of her conversion, government security forces detained her and locked her into a metal shipping container stranded in the middle of the desert. They beat, tortured, and sexually assaulted her. They forced her to renounce her church membership. Dehab was finally able to escape and fled over harsh terrain to Sudan, and then on to the United States, where she has a relative who is a U.S. citizen.

Dehab applied for asylum four months after arriving in the United States. At her asylum interview, a U.S. asylum officer told her that though he knew all about the terrible persecution in Eritrea, and though she met the substantive definition of a refugee under the law, he could not grant asylum because Dehab did not have a passport reflecting her date of entry to the United States, and therefore could not prove that her asylum application had been filed within a year of that date.

As a result of the filing deadline, Dehab's case – which could have been resolved at the asylum office level – was then put through the immigration court removal process. The resolution of her case was further delayed because a hearing date was not available for another year. During that year, Dehab lived in a state of limbo.

Dehab's court hearing, which required the presence of an immigration judge and a DHS trial attorney, lasted the entire day. Only two hours of the hearing were devoted to the merits of Dehab's asylum claim. The overwhelming majority of the hearing time focused on the filing deadline and whether Dehab could prove the date she arrived in the United States by "clear and convincing evidence."

Ultimately, the immigration judge denied Dehab's asylum claim even though he found her testimony credible and compelling and concluded that she met the "refugee" definition. He even found that she met the higher burden of proof for withholding of removal. But he said that he could not grant her asylum because he did not believe that her compliance with the filing deadline had been established by "clear and convincing" evidence – despite the fact that Dehab submitted three affidavits and documentary evidence proving that she had been in the United States for less than a year before she filed her asylum application.

Dehab now works full time at a gas station in Maryland and attends community college on a part time basis. She applied for financial aid, but her college informed her that she was not eligible because she only had withholding of removal rather than a more permanent form of immigration status. Dehab would like to attend college full time and become a radiologist, but she cannot afford the tuition.

The path of Dehab's asylum request illustrates many of the inefficiencies caused by the filing deadline. Because of the filing deadline, Dehab's case – which could have been resolved promptly at the asylum office level – was put into the removal process and had to go through the additional process of an immigration court hearing. That process took another year, and required the expenditure of additional governmental resources – including the time of an immigration judge, a DHS trial attorney and immigration court clerks. And in the end, Dehab, a credible refugee as confirmed by the immigration court, was denied asylum and left with a limited form of protection from deportation that is undermining her ability to integrate into and contribute to this country.

A. Diverting Time at the Asylum Office Level and Immigration Courts

> *"One year deadline cases can be extremely time-consuming, even before you get to the merits of the case. It's like two completely separate adjudications."*
>
> - Former U.S. Asylum Officer [50]

As a result of the asylum filing deadline, each asylum officer and each immigration judge handling each asylum case must devote time to assessing whether the individual asylum seeker filed the asylum application within one year of his or her entry to the United States. Even when applications are timely filed, the asylum officer or the immigration judge must still elicit "clear and convincing evidence" that this procedural hurdle has been cleared.[51] This assessment can take a significant amount of time in the many cases in which applicants do not file their applications within a year of arrival – as well as in those cases in which applicants do not have documentary proof of their arrival dates.

In fact, prior to the enactment of the one-year asylum filing deadline, senior immigration officials were concerned that a filing deadline would divert time that should be devoted to assessing the substance of asylum claims. As one official explained in February 1996, "[A] deadline will gum up the process and have us spinning around an issue – when a person entered the country – which is difficult to prove, rather than just hearing the claim and getting to the substance.[52]

According to U.S. government statistics, in 100,411 affirmative asylum cases – which amount to about 32% of all affirmative asylum applications filed from FY 1998 to FY 2009 – the applications triggered filing deadline scrutiny.[53] (The many reasons that genuine refugees are often unable to file their applications within a year of entry are discussed in Section IV of this report.) Thus in tens of thousands of cases, asylum officers have had to – and will have to – devote significant amounts of time to eliciting facts and conducting an assessment of whether the individual might be barred from asylum or might qualify for an exception to the filing deadline. Filing deadline inquiries can be complex and time consuming. The asylum office training manual and regulations make clear that these cases require a close examination of a long list of technical and substantive issues, such as:

- When did the applicant arrive in the U.S?[54]
- Can the applicant prove his date of arrival by "clear and convincing evidence"?[55]
- If the applicant does not have documentary proof of entry, is his testimony regarding his arrival credible considering "the totality of the circumstances"?[56]
- If the applicant cannot prove his date of arrival, can he show that he was in another country less than one year prior to applying?[57]
- Did U.S. Citizenship and Immigration Services receive the asylum application within one year of the applicant's arrival?[58]
- If the application was not timely received, can the applicant prove by "clear and convincing documentary evidence" that he mailed it within one year of his arrival?[59]
- If the application was not timely mailed or received, does the applicant qualify for an exception?[60]
- Did the applicant experience "changed circumstances" such as worsened conditions in the applicant's country of nationality, changes in the applicant's personal circumstances, or changes in U.S. law?[61]
- Are the changed circumstances "material" to the applicant's eligibility for asylum?[62]
- Alternatively, did the applicant experience "extraordinary circumstances" such as serious illness, legal disability, ineffective assistance of counsel, maintenance of lawful status in the United States, or unsuccessful attempts to timely file?[63]

- Were the extraordinary circumstances "directly related" to the failure to timely file?[64]
- Can the applicant prove the existence of an exception with documentary evidence and credible testimony "to the satisfaction" of the asylum officer?[65]
- If the applicant does qualify for an exception, did he or she file "within a reasonable time" of the changed or extraordinary circumstances?[66]
- If the applicant did not file within a reasonable time after changed circumstances, can he or she establish that he or she was not aware of the change until after it occurred?[67]

Asylum officers have a limited amount of time to assess each individual case. On average, they have about four hours to (1) review an applicant's file and check databases; (2) conduct the asylum interview; (3) update the Refugees, Asylum, and Parole System (RAPS) database; (4) write a decision with legal analysis and country conditions citations; and (5) prepare a decision letter.[68]

During this time, asylum officers must ask the questions and conduct the research that will enable them to assess whether the individual has a well founded fear of persecution, otherwise satisfies the "refugee" standards, and is credible – and whether he or she might be barred from asylum due to any wrongdoing. But because the one-year deadline is an issue in so many cases, valuable time that could be better spent addressing the substance of an asylum claim is instead devoted to sorting through this procedural obstacle. As one former asylum officer told Human Rights First in an interview, "One-year deadline cases can be extremely time consuming, even before you get to the merits of the case. It's like two completely separate adjudications."[69]

In addition to consuming valuable interview time, the filing deadline also consumes significant training time for asylum officers. The training manual for the filing deadline is a 32-page document.[70] A full lesson lasting approximately four hours – and provided to each officer – is devoted to this training.[71] Indeed, given the serious consequences resulting from a mistaken filing deadline

determination, if anything, more time is needed to train officers – and immigration judges – to handle these assessments accurately and effectively.

The questions and research relating to the asylum filing deadline can divert time in immigration court proceedings as well. Like asylum officers, immigration judges must conduct technical and substantive inquiries to establish that an asylum seeker filed within a year of entry – or if he or she did not, to decide whether the individual qualifies for an exception and filed within a "reasonable time" given that exception. Some immigration judges even conduct separate hearings to assess whether the individual is barred from asylum based on the filing deadline. Attorneys may draft legal briefs or portions of legal briefs to address issues relating to the filing deadline, including timeliness of the filing, eligibility for an exception, and the timing of any filing given an exception. Sometimes separate witnesses are called to testify during immigration court hearings to address issues relating to the timing of the filing, the reasons for a late filing, or eligibility for an exception. This additional time spent on a procedural issue, rather than the merits of a refugee determination, constitutes a waste of resources and an additional burden on the already under-staffed and backlogged immigration courts.

For example:

- **The filing deadline led to extra briefing and delay in the adjudication of the asylum case of a woman with well founded fears of persecution in Afghanistan.** The judge ultimately agreed with her *pro bono* counsel that she was eligible for asylum and met a number of exceptions to the one-year filing deadline such that her claim was not time-barred.[72] However, the judge also knew that the DHS trial attorney might appeal a grant based on the filing deadline. Accordingly, the judge required extra briefing on the filing deadline issue, requested that the parties discuss and try to reach an agreement on the issue out of court, and scheduled an additional hearing to deal with the issue before reaching the merits of the asylum case. The filing deadline required more hours of court time than would have been needed otherwise and also led to a delay of an additional month during which the judge was drafting a written decision that could withstand an appeal on that issue.

- **Asylum request of torture survivor from Guinea not granted for two years, after initial rejection at the asylum office level based on the filing deadline.** The pro-democracy political activist fled to the United States after being detained and tortured by Guinean government officials because of his peaceful political activities.[73] He filed for asylum within a year of entering the United States, but the asylum office rejected his request for asylum based on the filing deadline after concluding that he could not prove the date he entered the country. The case was referred into immigration court proceedings. The immigration court required additional briefing on the filing deadline issues, and the judge concluded the merits hearing by telling the applicant that he needed time to consider the arguments made by his *pro bono* attorneys regarding the one-year filing deadline. Two and a half months later, the judge issued a decision granting asylum, finding that the political activist had indeed filed his asylum application in a timely manner. The judge granted asylum nearly two years after the activist had originally submitted his application.

B. Pushing Asylum Seekers into the Immigration Court System Wastes Governmental Resources

"The immigration courts have too few immigration judges and support staff, including law clerks, for the workload for which they are responsible .... The shortage of immigration judges and law clerks has led to very heavy caseloads per judge and a lack of sufficient time for judges to properly consider the evidence and formulate well-reasoned opinions in each case."

- Karen Grisez, Chair of the American Bar Association (ABA) Commission on Immigration[74]

Since the filing deadline went into effect, over 53,400 asylum seekers have had their requests for asylum rejected by the asylum office based on the deadline and not on the merits of their cases.[75] As a result, thousands of asylum cases have been put into the overloaded immigration court system. Some (though not all) of those cases could have been – and would have been – resolved at the asylum office level through a grant of asylum if the filing deadline did not exist. The asylum office does not track these cases after they are referred to the immigration courts, and the immigration courts do not track filing deadline data in their statistics. However, according to a recent analysis of DHS data by Georgetown University Law professors, from April 1998, when the deadline went into effect, through June 2009, it is likely that DHS has rejected more than 15,000 asylum applications involving more than 21,000 refugees -- and potentially more if family members are included -- who otherwise would have been granted asylum without the need for further litigation if there were no filing deadline.[76]

Human Rights First's own case data confirms that legitimate refugees are being shifted into removal proceedings after being rejected at the asylum office based on the filing deadline. From 2005 to 2008, Human Rights First took on the cases of 35 asylum seekers whose applications were initially rejected by the asylum office based on the filing deadline.[77] While 9 of these cases remain pending, 26 of the asylum seekers have been granted asylum or withholding of removal by a judge in our immigration courts – confirming that they are indeed credible refugees who have suffered persecution and/or have well-founded fears of persecution.[78] Thus, of the Human Rights First cases that were rejected by the asylum office based on the filing deadline, 74% have already been granted asylum or, as a result of the filing deadline, withholding of removal. As the rest of these cases are still pending, this success rate will certainly increase (given Human Rights First's success rate of over 90% in asylum cases) as more of these cases are resolved. This means that if there were no filing deadline all of these cases which have been adjudicated by our immigration courts so far could have been resolved more quickly at the asylum office level without the need for immigration court removal proceedings.

When a case is rejected by the asylum office based on the filing deadline, it is referred into the removal process and placed into immigration court removal proceedings. The court process – which is an adversarial process – involves a significantly greater use of government resources. At the asylum office, an asylum seeker is interviewed by a single officer of the U.S. Department of Homeland Security. The interview takes place over the course of a few hours, at most, on a single day and the government is not represented by a trial attorney because the interview takes place in a non-adversarial setting. Immigration court hearings are presided over by individual immigration judges – who are part of the Executive Office for Immigration Review (EOIR), an arm of the U.S. Department of Justice. Additional government employees are also present. The U.S. Department of Homeland Security is represented by a "trial attorney" who is employed by Immigration and Customs Enforcement (ICE). The judge has a court clerk present during the hearing, and if needed an interpreter is also present during the hearing, all at government expense.

Not only do immigration court proceedings involve the time of several government employees, but they also

require at least two different hearings. In immigration court, an asylum seeker must first attend a brief "master calendar" hearing, used for pleading and scheduling purposes. He or she must then attend a much longer "merits" hearing, where the substance of the claim is heard. Complicated asylum cases may require multiple master calendar and merits hearing dates before the immigration court issues a decision. For example, among Human Rights First cases, 90% of asylum cases originally referred into immigration court removal proceedings based on the deadline (but ultimately granted asylum or withholding of removal – confirming that these individuals were indeed refugees with well-founded fears of persecution) required more than one merits hearing date, and 38% required three or more merits hearing dates.[79]

Cases that are referred into removal proceedings can be significantly delayed, as they will wait months and often longer for hearings to be conducted and completed. These delays have only been exacerbated by the underfunded, under-staffed, and backlogged immigration court system. According to a June 2010 study from the Transactional Records Access Clearinghouse (TRAC) at Syracuse University, the average wait time for an immigration court hearing is 459 days.[80] Delays are even longer in some areas: in March 2010, the average wait time for a hearing was 612 days in the Boston immigration court, and 713 days in the Los Angeles immigration court.[81]

An analysis of Human Rights First's caseload also confirms that asylum cases can be significantly delayed when they are rejected by an asylum officer based on the filing deadline and referred into removal proceedings. In the four-year period analyzed, half of Human Rights First's filing deadline cases that were granted at the asylum office level were completed within three months, and two-thirds were granted within six months. Only 16% of these cases took more than a year. In contrast, in our immigration court filing deadline cases only 15% of asylum grants occurred within one year of filing for asylum. In fact, one-third of Human Rights First filing deadline cases that were referred into immigration court removal proceedings took more than two years to complete and 15% required more than three years to complete.

Many of Human Rights First's filing deadline cases demonstrate the inefficiencies and delays caused by the filing deadline. In the cases listed below (and in many of the other case examples in this report), asylum applicants who were ultimately found by U.S. adjudicators to have well founded fears, or to face a clear probability, of persecution were only resolved after an extended immigration court removal proceeding. These cases could have been granted asylum at the initial asylum office level – saving countless hours of government time and corresponding resources – if they had not been rejected under the filing deadline.

For example:

- **A torture survivor from Togo was granted asylum only after a three-year process due to the filing deadline.** After being detained by the Togolese military regime and tortured for seven months because of his peaceful political activities, this pro-democracy advocate from Togo fled to the United States. [82] After arriving in the United States he continued to suffer from severe post-traumatic stress disorder as a result of the seven months of detention and torture. He also did not speak English, had no way to support himself, and didn't even have a stable place to live. After a year and a half in the United States he filed for asylum. His request for asylum was rejected by the asylum officer based on the filing deadline, and his case was put into the immigration removal process. More than three years after he applied for asylum, the judge found that his application was not time-barred because he qualified for an exception to the deadline and the torture survivor was finally granted asylum.

- **The filing deadline delayed the asylum case for a gay man from Honduras who had been attacked and beaten due to his sexual orientation.** The man fled brutal persecution in Honduras after being attacked and beaten because of his sexual

orientation.[83] After arriving in the United States, he applied for protection from persecution. His asylum request was rejected by the asylum office based on the filing deadline after it concluded he could not prove the date he entered the United States by "clear and convincing" evidence. As a result, the asylum seeker's case was put into removal proceedings. Two years after he had initially applied, the man was finally granted protection. The immigration court concluded that the man had indeed complied with the filing deadline – that he had actually filed for asylum within one year of his arrival in the United States – and granted his request for asylum after finding that he also had a well-founded fear of persecution if forced to return to Honduras.

- **A Sierra Leonean woman who had suffered severe past persecution was initially denied asylum and was only granted asylum over a year later after an immigration court hearing.** The refugee from Sierra Leone, whose case was profiled in Section I above,[84] had her asylum request rejected at the asylum office, which concluded that she could not prove that she had been in the United States for less than one year because she did not have a passport showing her date of entry. As a result, her case was referred into immigration court proceedings. More than a year after she initially filed her asylum application, the judge acknowledged that she had filed within one year of entry and granted her asylum.

- **A woman from Guinea who suffered FGM and persecution because of her ethnicity was denied asylum because of the filing deadline.**[85] A U.S. corporation requested that she come to the United States, and arranged for her and her mother's travel, so she could take care of her severely disabled brother. The brother had been seriously injured while working on a fishing boat off the coast of Alaska; he lost all four limbs and suffered a brain injury. From the day that his sister and mother arrived in the United States they spent every waking hour caring for him. After more than one year in the United States, his sister began to learn some English and eventually heard about a non-profit legal services organization which helped her apply for asylum. At her asylum office interview, the asylum officer noted that her case fulfilled both the extraordinary and changed circumstances exceptions to the one-year filing deadline, but concluded that she had not filed within a reasonable time given those circumstances. The asylum office rejected her case, and it was referred into immigration court removal proceedings. At the second to last hearing for the mother, the judge described their situation as "tragic" and urged the DHS trial attorney to exercise prosecutorial discretion to not oppose a grant of asylum. In the fall of 2010, after briefing on the issue the judge granted asylum, finding that she quailified for exceptions to the deadline and filed within a reasonable time given those exceptions. Due to the filing deadline, the woman had to wait nearly two years for a resolution of her asylum case, during which time she has remained separated from her own two young daughters who remain in Guinea, at the risk of being subjected to female genital mutilation.

The filing deadline wastes government resources not only in the immigration courts, but also at the Board of Immigration Appeals (BIA). A review of four months of BIA asylum decisions revealed that about 19% of those cases were appealed in part because of the filing deadline – a total of over 660 cases in four months alone.[86] This review, of redacted BIA decisions provided by the Executive Office for Immigration Review to the National Immigrant Justice Center (NIJC) pursuant to a Freedom of Information Act Request, was conducted by Penn State Law's Center for Immigrants' Rights for, and with NIJC and Human Rights First. The BIA decisions were for January of each year from 2005 through 2008. Some of these cases could have been – and would have been – more efficiently resolved at an earlier stage of the asylum process but for the filing deadline. In fact, as noted above, the average wait time for an immigration court hearing is 459 days according to a June 2010 study.[87] Some examples of filing deadline cases before the BIA include:

- **Asylum case for refugee with well-founded fear of persecution delayed for at least two years by filing deadline litigation.** An immigration judge ruled that an asylum seeker was eligible for asylum and concluded that the asylum seeker's depression constituted an extraordinary circumstance warranting an exception to the filing deadline.[88] The immigration court's decision was issued in March 2004. The DHS attorney appealed the immigration judge's decision, arguing that the asylum seeker was barred by the deadline and not entitled to an exception. The BIA concluded that the asylum seeker had not met his burden of establishing that his failure to timely file was "directly related to" his depression. The BIA also stated that "lack of knowledge of the 1-year filing deadline and lack of English proficiency are not extraordinary circumstances." The BIA's decision – remanding the case back down to the immigration court for consideration of the asylum seeker's eligibility for withholding of removal – was issued in January 2006. While the BIA decision does not indicate the date the asylum application was filed (nor does it indicate the asylum seeker's nationality or any facts relating to his case), the DHS appeal to the BIA of the asylum grant based on the filing deadline added 22 months (and likely more than two years by the time the case was decided again by the immigration court on remand) to the course of the proceedings in this case. This additional expenditure of time occurred in a case involving an asylum seeker who had been determined by the immigration court to have a well-founded fear of persecution, a conclusion that the government attorney did not challenge on appeal.

- **A woman from Mauritania who was deemed likely to suffer persecution if returned was denied asylum based on the filing deadline and had to wait six and a half years for a final decision in her case.** The woman filed for asylum because she had suffered persecution and feared additional persecution in her home country due to her race.[89] A U.S. immigration court granted her withholding of removal and the government attorney did not appeal the withholding grant. However, the immigration court denied her application for asylum based on the filing deadline and the BIA affirmed that decision. The woman testified that she had entered the country seven months before she filed for asylum, but the court concluded that she did not submit enough evidence on this point. While the woman's application for asylum was stamped as received by U.S. immigration authorities in June 2001, the immigration court issued its decision in August 2005, and the BIA did not issue its decision affirming the filing deadline denial until January 2008. After six and a half years in our immigration system, the woman was left with a grant of withholding of removal instead of asylum—which requires a lower likelihood of harm—solely based on the filing deadline.

Ironically, instead of improving the asylum adjudication system, the one-year filing deadline has shifted the responsibility for resolving many asylum cases from the asylum office to the already overburdened immigration court system. The immigration court system – as has been widely reported – is already strapped for funding and human resources.[90] In fiscal year 2009, immigration courts completed 283,969 removal proceedings, over 1,100 per judge. Sixteen percent of these - 44,830 - were asylum adjudications. In fiscal year 2009 alone, over 4500 new filing deadline cases were rejected and referred into immigration court removal proceedings.[91]An August 2010 study conducted by the Transactional Records Clearinghouse (TRAC) at Syracuse University reported that the number of pending immigration court cases had reached an all-time high of 247,922. If the filing deadline were eliminated, asylum filing deadline cases that could otherwise be granted by the asylum office need not be shifted unnecessarily into removal proceedings, which should help alleviate the work load of the immigration courts.[92]

C. Providing Refugees with only a Temporary Status Undermines Integration and Separates Families

"The result is an almost impossible choice: live in safety while separated from one's family and their perilous life a world away, or join them in their peril and risk the probability of death or imprisonment."

- U.S. Court of Appeals for the Second Circuit on the choice facing a refugee granted withholding of removal but denied asylum based on the filing deadline [93]

In addition to the inefficiency of shifting asylum seekers into the immigration removal process, the one-year filing deadline also creates counterproductive results for the U.S. government by limiting the ability of some refugees to integrate, reunite their families, and rebuild their lives in this country. While some refugees are ordered deported based on the filing deadline, others are extended a limited form of protection from removal called withholding of removal, if they can meet the higher "clear probability of persecution" standard. (These different standards are described in Section I above.) These refugees are left in a kind of long term limbo. Since they are not granted asylum, their ability to integrate is limited. They are not authorized to apply for permanent resident status or U.S. citizenship.[94] Refugees who are only extended withholding of removal face significant hurdles in pursuing education, and often face difficulties obtaining stable employment since their status is not a permanent one and they have to regularly renew their work authorization.[95]

Sometimes when an asylum case implicates the filing deadline, the immigration judge or DHS trial attorney will encourage the applicant to "accept" withholding of removal – before he has even had the chance to present his case – to avoid an extended court hearing. In these cases, refugees are being asked to negotiate away their potential asylum eligibility – and their integration and family unity interests – in order to avoid the risk of the immigration judge granting no relief whatsoever.

Refugees who are left with only withholding of removal face a wide range of difficulties in securing employment, pursuing education, and otherwise rebuilding their lives. For example, Dehab, the Eritrean asylum seeker profiled above, was only granted withholding of removal, and as a result, has been unable to attend school full time because she is not eligible for scholarships or federal financial aid due to her lack of a more permanent immigration status. But she is not alone:

- **A refugee with withholding of removal could not pursue a job that requires travel outside the United States.** A gay man from Egypt applied for asylum after he had been in the United States for over a year.[96] In addition to fearing that he would be persecuted in Egypt for being gay, he also feared that he would be persecuted because of his recent conversion to Christianity. His attorneys believed he had a strong argument that his conversion constituted a changed circumstances exception to the filing deadline. The DHS trial attorney offered to agree to a grant of withholding of removal, but only if the man would agree to forego his right to a full asylum hearing; the trial attorney threatened that if he decided to insist on a hearing to try to get asylum, the trial attorney would automatically appeal any favorable decision he received from the immigration judge. At this point, the man's case had been pending in court for two years. He accepted the withholding of removal "settlement." But this status undermined his ability to advance his career. Recently, the man was offered a non-military position as an Arabic translator in the U.S. war effort in Iraq. He had to refuse, as he feared he would not be able to return to safety in the United States because as a "winner" of withholding of removal, he now has a final order of removal against him, meaning that if he ever travels outside the United States, he has no right to re-enter.

- **Refugee from Burundi who was kidnapped and tortured by rebels as a child was left in limbo due to filing deadline denial.** The refugee is a young man of the minority Twa ethnicity.[97] When he was a child, his mother was killed during a rebel attack and he was kidnapped by guerrilla forces who wanted him to serve as a child soldier. The guerrillas tortured the boy when he refused to fight. He fled to the United States and applied for asylum within a year of arrival. However, the young man had crossed the U.S.-Mexico border on foot, and the asylum officer rejected his case based on the filing deadline, concluding that he could not prove his date of entry. The asylum office referred the case into immigration court proceedings. At immigration court, the DHS trial attorney told the young man that she believed his story, but that she couldn't agree to asylum because he had not offered sufficient proof that he filed within a year of his arrival. Instead, she offered to accept a grant of withholding of removal if he would agree not to pursue his asylum case. The young man agreed to this "settlement" out of fear that he might not be granted asylum, or that the judge might grant him asylum but the DHS trial attorney would appeal, and in either case that he could be ordered deported back to persecution by the immigration court. With only this limited form of protection from removal, the young man was left in long-term legal limbo. As he was not granted asylum, he could never apply for lawful permanent resident status. In addition, about a year after he was granted withholding of removal, the young man was notified that he would be required by DHS to appear repeatedly at a DHS office for monitoring – leaving him in constant fear of deportation and also requiring him to repeatedly request that his employer let him take time off from work in order to comply with this requirement.

One of the most damaging consequences of withholding of removal is that it leaves refugee families separated. When the United States grants asylum to a refugee, that person – called an "asylee" under U.S. law – is allowed to file a request to bring his or her spouse and minor children to safety in the United States as derivative asylees.[98] When the United States accepts a refugee for resettlement in the United States, it also resettles that refugee's spouse and minor children.[99] Restoring the unity of refugee families benefits not only refugees and their families, but also the United States. Refugees who are reunited with their families are in a better position to recover from their trauma, rebuild their lives, and contribute to their communities economically and socially, lowering social costs for host states in the long term.[100]

However, when refugees receive withholding of removal but are denied asylum as result of the filing deadline, they do not have the chance to petition for their spouses and minor children to come to the United States as derivative asylees. These refugees – even though they have been found to meet the "refugee" definition and the higher burden of proof for withholding of removal – will remain separated from their spouses and young children indefinitely.

These families are not only separated, but in some cases these children and spouses are left stranded in difficult and even life-threatening situations abroad.   For example:

• **A persecuted businessman at risk of future persecution in Sri Lanka remains separated from his wife and children**. The Tamil business owner was persecuted, detained and threatened in Sri Lanka by both the Liberation Tigers of Tamil Eelam (LTTE) and the Sri Lankan government. The immigration court ruled that he had a "well founded fear of persecution" and also met the high "probability of persecution" standard for withholding of removal. But the court denied the man asylum, and the BIA affirmed, as he had filed more than a year after his arrival. The man said that he had not applied initially as he was waiting until the unrest at home would settle down so that he could return home to his family. The immigration court ruled that this was not an "extraordinary circumstance" which would excuse the delay in filing, and the BIA affirmed. The Second Circuit, citing its prior precedent, concluded that it did not have jurisdiction to review the filing deadline issue.[101] Because the business owner was denied asylum, he was not

able to bring his wife and children to safety in the United States – even though he faced a probability of persecution if he returned home. As the Second Circuit put it: "The result is an almost impossible choice: live in safety while separated from one's family and their perilous life a world away, or join them in their peril and risk the probability of death or imprisonment."[102]

• **A refugee from Zimbabwe who suffered from cancer was denied asylum based on the filing deadline and separated from his family.** The man suffered persecution in Zimbabwe and then fled to the United States.[103] After arriving, he was diagnosed with cancer and treated with chemotherapy.   The immigration court acknowledged that the man's illness had "a powerful impact on [his] psychological condition" and that he was severely depressed without his family. Even though the immigration court acknowledged that the refugee had been persecuted in Zimbabwe and would more likely than not suffer future persecution, it concluded that the refugee had waited too long after the cancer's remission to file for asylum, and was, as a result, barred from asylum by the filing deadline. While the refugee was extended withholding of removal, this form of limited relief did not allow him to bring his wife and children to the United States to reunite the family in this country.

• **A refugee from Bangladesh who sought asylum due to feared religious persecution by Islamist group was denied asylum based on the filing deadline.** [104] His family had been threatened by an Islamist group that had threatened to kill them and bomb their home because they belonged to the Ahmadi Muslim faith, a religious minority in Bangladesh. The immigration court ruled that the man was not eligible for an exception to the filing deadline, and denied his request for asylum, which left him with an order of removal to Bangladesh. The U.S. Court of Appeals for the Second Circuit reversed the denial of withholding of removal. The court found that the judge had failed to consider important evidence— specifically the letter that was sent to the man's wife by an Islamist group threatening to kill the family and destroy their home with a bomb—which established a likelihood of persecution if he were required to return. The court also noted the reports submitted by the asylum seeker that documented the persecution of members of the Ahmadi faith in Bangladesh. While the BIA has remanded the case back to the immigration court for re-consideration of a potential grant of withholding of removal, the denial of asylum remains. This means that the man will not be able to bring his wife and children to safety in the United States.

The Executive Committee of the UN High Commissioner for Refugees (UNHCR) has repeatedly emphasized the importance of ensuring the unity of refugee families and has urged states to adopt legislation protecting family unity.[105] Additionally, Article 23 of the International Covenant on Civil and Political Rights (ICCPR) – to which the United States is party – states that "[t]he family is the fundamental and natural group unit of society and is entitled to protection by society and the State."[106]

D. Refugees Deterred from Applying for Asylum

In some cases, genuine refugees have been deterred from applying for asylum because of the filing deadline. After hearing about the one-year filing deadline, some refugees have believed, incorrectly, that they cannot apply for asylum if they have lived in the United States for more than one year. They may not know about the exceptions to the filing deadline, or that they might be able to secure some more limited protection from removal even if they are time-barred from asylum. Human Rights First has interviewed refugees who mistakenly believed that they would not be eligible for any protection because of the filing deadline. In some cases, asylum seekers are simply given inaccurate advice – from community members, from well-meaning friends, from "notarios" or other non-lawyers who hold themselves out as lawyers, or from actual lawyers who lack familiarity

with this area of immigration law.

As a result, some legitimate refugees end up living in an undocumented status unnecessarily – an outcome that is not in the interest of the refugee or the interest of the U.S. government. In other cases, these asylum seekers only learn much later that they might in fact be eligible for an exception, so their asylum filing ends up being delayed even further because of the filing deadline and confusion relating to how it operates. For example:

- **Two disabled refugees from Colombia were told several years after they arrived in the United States that they had waited too long to apply for asylum and should not apply for protection due to the filing deadline.**[107] As a result, they did not file for protection until a few years later when someone else told them that it was still possible. They later met with an attorney from Human Rights First who found them *pro bono* counsel to help present their case to the Immigration Court. Their case remains pending and will require a showing that they qualify for an exception to the filing deadline, a burden made more onerous by the fact that they were deterred from filing earlier.

- **A refugee woman from Niger who fled forced marriage was advised that her asylum claim would be barred by the filing deadline and so did not file until later when she learned she might be eligible for an exception.** The young woman fled to the United States to escape from an imminent forced marriage and female genital mutilation (FGM).[108] In her first years in the United States, she suffered from debilitating asthma attacks and complications related to sickle cell anemia. She also gave birth to a daughter. Due to these medical issues, she dropped out of school, operating under the incorrect belief that her school, to which she planned to return, would renew her student visa. Upon her return to school, she discovered that her student visa had not been renewed (and had in fact expired) and consulted an immigration attorney who told her that she was not eligible for asylum because the filing deadline had already passed. As a result, she did not apply for asylum and, still fearful of return to Niger, continued to live in the United States without a legal status. Almost a year later, immigration officials arrested the woman in her home for overstaying her student visa. Human Rights First recruited *pro bono* attorneys to take on her case, and they submitted significant evidence to demonstrate her well-founded fears of persecution in Niger as well as evidence demonstrating her eligibility for an exception to the filing deadline given her illness, her pregnancy, the birth of her child, and the legal advice she was given concerning the filing deadline. The immigration judge stated that he believed that she was otherwise eligible for asylum, but suggested that it would be difficult for her to prove that she qualified for an exception to the filing deadline, so she accept withholding of removal rather than pursuing her asylum case in court. The woman was thus ultimately recognized as a refugee facing a clear probability of persecution, but was not granted asylum.

III. The System Has Measures to Combat Fraud, but the Deadline Bars Credible Refugees

"INS finally has sufficient staff and resources to stop the abuse and ensure that legitimate asylum seekers no longer pay the price for those who seek to misuse the system."

- Doris Meissner, then-INS Commissioner, about the asylum system before the implementation of the filing deadline.[109]

The filing deadline was proposed in the wake of concerns about abuse in the asylum system, but by the time it was enacted into law in 1996, U.S. immigration authorities had already overhauled the system in a reform effort that they later reported led to a steep drop in asylum applications. Ironically, in the years since the filing deadline was enacted, it has led the United States to deny or reject the asylum requests of many credible asylum seekers, as shown through this report's many case examples. Indeed, the filing deadline is not a necessary, appropriate, or effective tool for combating abuse and fraud. The deadline denies asylum to an individual regardless of whether he or she is a refugee with a well-founded fear of persecution or a person who has purposefully filed a fraudulent application. The U.S. asylum system and U.S. law contain many measures – which are detailed below – to help identify fraud and prevent individuals who constitute a threat to the United States from receiving asylum in this country. Individuals who file fraudulent asylum claims can be investigated and prosecuted. Individuals whose testimony is appropriately determined not to be credible can be – and are routinely – denied asylum. A filing deadline is not needed to deny asylum to fraudulent or not credible asylum applicants. But it is causing legitimate asylum seekers to be denied asylum by the United States.

A. Congressional Concerns About Abuse – But the System Had Already Been Reformed

Congress passed the one-year filing deadline in the wake

of concerns that the asylum system was being abused by individuals who were filing fraudulent asylum claims. Rep. Robert Franks (R-NJ), when introducing a bill aimed at reform of the asylum process, asserted that the asylum system had "spun out of control" and was "easy to exploit." [110] In the run-up to passage of the Illegal Immigration Reform and Immigrant Responsibility Act of 1996 (IIRIRA), several Congress members voiced their concerns about the exploitation of the asylum system by individuals who sought asylum after being taken into custody within the United States and put into deportation proceedings.[111] Given this concern, the original Senate version of the bill did not apply the time limit to affirmative applications. As Senator Orrin Hatch (R-UT) noted, "[t]he Senate provisions had established a 1-year time limit only on defensive claims of asylum, that is, those raised for the first time in deportation proceedings ...."[112] The Senate version of the bill also provided for a "good cause" exception to the filing deadline, which Senator Hatch said would be largely encompassed by the two exceptions ultimately passed.[113]

Meanwhile, President Clinton's administration was already taking steps to address the concerns about the U.S. asylum system. The former INS had initiated its own major reform process and began implementing those reforms in 1995. Previously, an individual could apply for asylum in the U.S. and – because of the substantial delays and backlogs in the system – stay in the United States for years while awaiting adjudication by the asylum office. After applying for asylum, the individual was also given work authorization. By 1994, the number of people in the asylum office's backlog exceeded 425,000.[114]

Under the revamped system, individuals who filed asylum applications were interviewed and issued decisions by asylum officers much more quickly – generally within 60 days.[115] Those who were not granted asylum were, and generally still are, promptly referred into deportation proceedings, now called removal proceedings. In addition to improving the timeline for resolving asylum cases, the reforms increased the number of asylum officers to ensure that cases could be adjudicated more quickly. The new regulations also eliminated the automatic grant of work authorization to individuals who file for asylum, thus eliminating one obvious incentive for fraudulent asylum applications.[116]

In early 1996, then INS Commissioner Doris M. Meissner described the reforms as a "dramatic success" that had "fixed a broken system."[117] Addressing the question of fraudulent asylum claims, Ms. Meissner said that the "INS finally has sufficient staff and resources to stop the abuse and ensure that legitimate asylum seekers no longer pay the price for those who seek to misuse the system."[118] U.S. immigration authorities released statistical data that reflected a sharp drop in affirmative asylum filings following the implementation of their reform measures – from 122,589 applications in 1994 down to 53,255 applications after the regulations went into effect in 1995.[119] Similarly, asylum applications for immigrants already placed in deportation proceedings decreased from 21,811 to 15,322 during the same time period.[120] The INS also reported that it had doubled its annual rate of adjudication – meaning that those without meritorious cases were being referred by the asylum office into immigration court deportation proceedings (now called removal proceedings) much more quickly, helping to deter fraudulent filings.[121] Five years later, the INS issued additional statistics which it concluded confirmed that the reforms were still working. New asylum claims had dropped 75 percent, from 127,129 in 1993 to 30,261 in 1999. Conversely, the asylum office's approval rate had increased from 15 percent to 38 percent in the same time frame, which the immigration authorities believed indicated that fewer fraudulent claims were being filed.[122]

Despite the INS's reforms to the asylum system, Congress passed IIRIRA – which included the one-year bar to asylum - in 1996. Ms. Meissner called the legislation "the quintessential fighting-the-last-war scenario."[123] She expressed particular concern about the imposition of a filing deadline, calling it an "overreaction" and "an idea that is born of assumptions about a system in the past."[124] Officials from both the Department of Justice and then - INS believed that the 1995 reforms had addressed the flaws in the asylum system, and that a filing deadline would be a step backward.[125] Then Deputy Attorney General Jamie S. Gorelick warned that the proposed changes "would dramatically transform the character of asylum proceedings at the current time" and some would even "have the unintended result of reversing significant progress that we have made in the asylum area."[126]

B. Anti-Fraud and Security Safeguards in the Asylum System

The U.S. asylum system and U.S. law contain many measures that are specifically aimed at, and closely tailored to, weeding out fraudulent filings in the system. The Illegal Immigration Reform and Immigrant Responsibility Act itself contained strict security provisions, including a requirement that identity checks be conducted against federal government databases and records for all individuals applying for asylum.[127] Since then, many additional measures have been added.

Outlined below are just some of the mechanisms that are designed to protect the immigration and asylum systems from abuse:

■ **Asylum Applications Signed Under Penalty of Perjury.** When the INS overhauled the asylum system in 1995, it revised the asylum application form to require both the asylum applicant and the individual preparing the application to sign the application "under penalty of perjury" to ensure that there would be "appropriate consequences for making false statements."[128]

■ **Fraudulent Applicants Permanently Barred**
IIRIRA included a provision that permanently barred anyone who files a fraudulent asylum application from receiving any immigration benefit – meaning that such an individual would never be able to work legally in the United States, or to receive permanent lawful resident status here.[129]

■ **Fraudulent Filers, Preparers, and Attorneys Can Be Prosecuted.** Individuals who seek to defraud the immigration and asylum system can be and have been prosecuted.[130] Unscrupulous "notarios" and attorneys take advantage of immigrants by untruthfully telling them they are eligible for certain benefits and then preparing fraudulent applications – including asylum applications – for large fees. To facilitate prosecution of fraudulent filers, USCIS is a member of ICE's Document and Benefit Fraud Task Force, which coordinates with U.S. Attorney's Offices to identify and prosecute fraudulent immigration benefit claims.[131] Charges have been brought against such preparers in many states, including California, New York, Texas, Florida, and Arizona.[132]

■ **Multiple Identity and Security Checks for Asylum Seekers in DHS and other government databases.** IIRIRA requires that each asylum seeker's identity be checked in a series of federal databases.[133] These checks can help identify fraudulent cases as well as any individual who might present a security risk. These checks include:
(1) Interagency Border Inspection System – a multi-agency database including information on immigration violations, criminal violations, and terrorist threats;
(2) U.S. Visitor and Immigrant Status Indicator technology – a DHS database with biometric information on foreign nationals entering and exiting the United States;

(3) Consular Consolidated Database – a Department of State database with information on visa applications and prior travel history; and
(4) Deportable Alien Control System – a DHS database on aliens who have been detained or put in removal proceedings.[134]

Additionally, U.S. adjudicators may request records on asylum applicants from INTERPOL, the international police organization.[135]

■ **FBI Fingerprint and Name Checks for Asylum Applicants.** Asylum officers and immigration judges are not authorized to grant asylum until the applicant's fingerprints have been run through the FBIQUERY database.[136] Asylum applicants' names are also automatically checked against the FBI name database.[137]

■ **Office of Fraud Detection and National Security.** USCIS's Office of Fraud Detection and National Security aids in identifying fraudulent asylum claims by training asylum officers and providing technical support.[138] Through this office, asylum officers may refer suspected fraudulent applications to ICE for criminal investigation and prosecution.[139]

■ **Forensic Testing of Documents.** Documents provided in support of asylum claims are often sent to DHS's Forensic Document Laboratory. There, technicians analyze the documents' authenticity and, in the case of official documents, compare them to the lab's library of foreign travel and identity documents.[140]

More can certainly be done to address concerns of fraud in the immigration system and to prosecute cases of fraudulent preparers. Many advocates have called for a federal law making it a felony for a "notario," attorney, or other preparer to defraud someone under the U.S. immigration system.[141] Catholic Charities and *pro bono* attorneys from the law firm of Bryan Cave LLP have petitioned the Federal Trade Commission to consider enforcement actions against fraudulent preparers through consumer protection statutes.[142] Meanwhile, the American Bar Association's Commission on Immigration recently launched a campaign to provide attorneys and others with training and resources for civil suits against fraudulent preparers under state consumer protection laws.[143]

Finally, and importantly, adjudicators do not need a filing deadline to deny asylum protection to fraudulent applicants. An asylum applicant does not enjoy any presumption of credibility and under the law will be denied if the adjudicator does not find her claim truthful.[144]

IV. Refugees Denied Exceptions to the Filing Deadline

"I wish I had known about the filing deadline. . . . I don't know what will happen in the future. I don't feel secure."

- An Eritrean asylum seeker who was denied asylum based on the filing deadline[145]

In cases where an asylum applicant has not applied for asylum within one year of arrival, or cannot establish that he or she applied within one year of arrival, the applicant may be able to secure an exemption from the filing deadline if he or she can demonstrate "either the existence of changed circumstances which materially affect the applicant's eligibility for asylum or extraordinary circumstances relating to the delay in filing...."[146] The Senate version of the filing deadline legislation had actually contained a "good cause exception," which was not ultimately included in the final law. Senator Orrin Hatch, one of the deadline's main proponents, stated that "circumstances covered by the Senate's good cause exception will likely be covered by either the changed circumstances exception of the extraordinary circumstances exception," and that "the way in which the time limit was rewritten in the conference report – with the two exceptions specified – was intended to provide adequate protections to those with legitimate claims of asylum."[147] He went on to reiterate his commitment to avoid deporting refugees, "particularly for technical deficiencies."[148]

Despite the existence of these exceptions – in both statute and regulations – over half of applicants with filing deadline issues have had their asylum cases rejected by the U.S. asylum office. From 1998 to 2009, 100,411 cases were identified as triggering the filing deadline at the asylum office. Of those, 54,300 cases, or 53 percent, have been rejected based on the filing deadline and referred into the immigration court removal process.[153] These statistics do not reveal how many of these asylum seekers were later determined to be eligible for an exception (or should have been found to be eligible for an exception). However, the percentage of cases rejected based on the filing deadline increased sharply during the first years of its implementation – from 37% in 1998, to 39% in 1999, 42% in 2000, and 51% in 2001 – leading to concerns that the filing deadline was being applied in an increasingly narrow manner as, over time, the existence of a filing deadline became a "bureaucratic routine."[154] Since the filing deadline was instituted, many legal experts have expressed concern that some asylum officers and immigration judges are applying the exceptions too narrowly, sometimes in direct contravention of Congressional intent.[155]

While conducting research for this report, Human Rights First learned of many cases in which genuine refugees were denied asylum under the filing deadline despite

---

The Exceptions:

The relevant federal regulations contain a non-exhaustive list of scenarios that might constitute changed or extraordinary circumstances.[149] Changed circumstances include, but are not limited to, changes in conditions in the applicant's country of origin, changes in applicable U.S. law, new conditions which make an individual a refugee sur place, and the loss of a qualifying relationship to another asylum applicant who listed the individual as a dependent.[150] Extraordinary circumstances could be serious illness or mental or physical disability, legal disability including being an unaccompanied minor, ineffective assistance of counsel, the maintenance of another type of immigration status, prior attempts to timely file for asylum, and the death or serious illness of an applicant's family member or legal representative.[151] As both the regulation and its history make clear, these examples are not meant to be exhaustive – they are simply some examples.[152]

having common, understandable reasons for their late filings. In some cases, despite the existence of an exception that should have excused the late filing, the adjudicator still denied asylum based on the filing deadline. In some of these cases, adjudicators denied an exception because the purported reason for the late filing was not specifically listed among the examples of circumstances that could qualify for an exception in the "non-exhaustive" list provided in the regulations. In other cases, adjudicators concluded that the exceptions did not cover the asylum seeker's circumstances. These refugees who were denied exceptions to the filing deadline include: refugees who suffered from post-traumatic stress disorder (PTSD) or depression following their traumatic experiences; refugees whose cases involved gender, sexual orientation, or potential social stigma; refugees who were waiting for conditions to improve so that they could return home; refugees who lacked knowledge of asylum law; refugees who lacked effective representation; and refugees who otherwise qualified for an exception to the filing deadline but were considered to have not filed within a "reasonable period" of time after that exception occurred.

A. Refugees Who Suffer from Post-Traumatic Stress and Other Serious Psychological Disorders Denied Asylum

In many cases, asylum seekers who suffer from Post-Traumatic Stress Disorder (PTSD) and other psychological disorders are found ineligible for an exception to the filing deadline. PTSD is a psychological disorder experienced by many survivors of rape, assault, torture, and other life-threatening events.[156] Because many refugees have fled persecution in their home countries, PTSD occurs at a high rate among this population – up to 82 percent in one study.[157] Individuals with PTSD often suffer distressing flashbacks and nightmares, and can have difficulty remembering or discussing their past experiences – a necessity in seeking asylum.[158] Because asylum applications require applicants to articulate their past experiences - and be

questioned about them - the asylum process can be re-traumatizing for these refugees, so they may not be able to engage in the asylum process until their health has improved. Dr. Allen Keller, the Director of the Bellevue/NYU Program for Survivors of Torture, has explained that:

> Generally, the most deserving asylum applicants are unable to speak about their persecution immediately after they arrive in the United States. Victims of torture, and others who suffer from Post-Traumatic Stress Disorder, have great difficulty relating their stories both to their representatives and to U.S. authorities until they have had time to recover from their trauma.[159]

Refugees have also been found to suffer from major depression and generalized anxiety disorders, further impeding their ability to apply for asylum.[160]

During floor discussions about the filing deadline, Senator Hatch informed the Senate that the extraordinary circumstances exception "could include, for instance, physical or mental disability...."[161] The regulations on the deadline specifically identify as an exception "[s]erious illness or mental or physical disability, including any effects of persecution or violent harm suffered in the past, during the one-year period after arrival."[162]

Even though individuals who are suffering from PTSD or other psychological disorders should be afforded exceptions to the filing deadline, many still find their cases denied or delayed as a result of the filing deadline. In some cases, adjudicators point to an applicant's ability to perform other tasks in their lives – such as maintain a job, take care of his or her children, or attend church - to conclude that the applicant had the capacity to file for asylum. This analysis reflects a fundamental misunderstanding about the nature of trauma and PTSD. As one medical expert has explained: "Traumatized people often avoid people, places, and activities that are unwelcome reminders of the original traumatic event or events. In other words there is specificity to the avoidance, and also to the associated disability. By and large, such people may function quite well so long as they are not reminded of the original event."[163] In other cases, adjudicators have concluded that asylum seekers have not met their burden of "proving" that the late filing was "directly related" to their condition or that they suffered from the condition during the entire time when they could otherwise have filed for asylum.[164] These decisions sometimes reflect a mistaken expectation that a medical professional can attest to the mental state of an individual not at the time the medical professional conducted the exam, but at some point in time years earlier.

Some examples of refugees whose asylum requests were rejected, denied, or delayed based on the filing deadline even though they were suffering from PTSD or other psychological disorders include:

- **A rape survivor's asylum application was initially rejected and delayed for three years based on the filing deadline.** A woman from The Gambia was subjected to FGM as a child and then forced to marry an abusive husband.[165] For two decades, the woman's husband brutally raped and beat her. She tried to escape from him many times, sometimes even crossing into neighboring countries, but each time her husband found her and forced her to return to him. Finally, the woman was able to flee to the United States with the help of her sister. Deeply traumatized, the woman continued to move frequently to avoid detection. After several years, she came into contact with Catholic Social Services, who told her that she may be eligible for asylum. The woman filed for asylum with the help of *pro bono* attorneys. She included with her application a medical evaluation from a doctor that diagnosed her with PTSD and Major Depressive Disorder. The asylum office rejected her asylum request under the filing deadline, and the immigration judge also denied asylum based on the filing deadline. The judge concluded that the woman's PTSD did not merit an exception based on the "totality of [her] life activities," including "the ability to make appropriate life decisions, to have ongoing employment,

[and] to be able to relocate to take advantage of opportunities." He also declined to rely on the doctor's evaluation because the doctor was not treating the woman on a continuing basis and had also conducted evaluations for other asylum applicants. The woman appealed to the BIA, which reversed the decision, finding her eligible for an exception to the filing deadline and granting her request for asylum nearly three years after she applied.

- **A woman from Turkmenistan who was tortured for studying the Bible and suffered ongoing effects of torture was denied exception to the filing deadline.** The woman was born into a Muslim family and many of her extended family members were arrested and tortured for teaching about Islam.[166] Her son converted to Christianity and was tortured to death because of his conversion. The woman also converted to Christianity and fled to the United States after being detained and tortured twice for studying the Bible. Once in the United States, she did not apply for asylum right away because she was suffering from extreme depression, panic attacks, and social isolation. She attempted suicide on one occasion and was placed on psychiatric medication. Due to the ongoing effects of the past persecution she suffered, she did not learn how to apply for asylum until more than one year after she arrived in the United States. She filed for asylum soon after she learned about it, but the case was rejected based on the filing deadline. Her case was then referred into removal proceedings and is currently pending before the immigration courts.

- **A Kenyan woman diagnosed with PTSD and depression was denied an exception to the filing deadline because she was able to attend church during time she suffered from health problems.** A Kenyan woman who sought asylum based on a fear of FGM applied for asylum after her filing deadline had passed.[167] In support of her asylum request, she submitted a psychological evaluation from a medical professional diagnosing her with Post-Traumatic Stress Disorder and Major Depressive Disorder. The asylum office rejected her asylum request based on the filing deadline stating that her Post-Traumatic Stress Disorder and Major Depressive Disorder did not contribute to her delay in filing because she was able to attend church during the same time period. Prior to her immigration hearing, the DHS trial attorney offered the woman withholding of removal. Rather than risk being deported by the immigration court, the woman accepted withholding of removal and withdrew her asylum application.[168]

B. Refugees in Cases Involving Gender, Sexual Orientation, or Social Stigma Denied Exceptions to Deadline

"I had never heard of the word 'asylum' before."
> - a young woman who feared "honor killing" in Jordan and only learned about asylum several years after arriving in the United States.[169]

Some refugees do not file for asylum within a year of arrival because they do not know that they might be eligible for asylum or because they may believe that the facts relating to their fears of persecution would lead them to be ostracized. For example, women who have fled persecution relating to honor killings, forced marriage, domestic violence, FGM or other gender-related persecution may be unaware that they may qualify for what is popularly referred to as "political asylum."[170] This confusion has only been compounded by the U.S. government's continuing failure to issue regulations clarifying the interpretation of the "particular social group" category and "nexus" requirement of U.S asylum law.[171] Women who have suffered these harms may only learn about their potential eligibility for asylum after their filing deadlines have passed.[172] Similarly, individuals who suffered persecution due to their sexual or gender identity, or their HIV status may not know that they might be eligible for asylum on those grounds.[173] Indeed, until 1990, being gay or lesbian was a basis for denying

admission to the United States under immigration law,[174] and individuals who are HIV positive required waivers to enter the country until 2010.[175]

Women often flee forms of persecution in their home countries that are related to their gender, such as rape, female genital mutilation, honor killings, domestic violence, or forced abortions. The personal and social shame experienced by these women can be acute. Gender-related forms of persecution are often difficult for women to talk about, particularly for women who come from cultures where they would be subject to further persecution or scorn if the nature of their mistreatment became public knowledge.[176]

Refugees who have suffered persecution due to their sexual or gender identity – as well as refugees who are HIV-positive – often face considerable social stigma or risk of harm by their families or other communities. When they first arrive in the United States, these refugees often must seek shelter and support from extended family or other community members from their home countries. Fearing the loss of this assistance, and the loss of community more broadly, refugees may fear disclosing their sexual orientation, gender identity, or HIV status – making it difficult to seek asylum based on these facts.[177]

As a result of these fears, as well as misinformation about potential asylum eligibility, some refugees do not file for asylum within a year of their arrival and have been denied asylum based on the filing deadline. For example:

- **A victim of trafficking and rape was denied asylum based on filing deadline.** An Albanian teenager was kidnapped, raped and battered while plans were made to traffic her into prostitution.[178] She was able to escape her traffickers, but feared she would be at risk if she returned to Albania. She fled to the United States, where she applied for asylum, while still a minor, thirteen months after entering the country. In support of her asylum application, she submitted a psychological evaluation diagnosing her with Post-Traumatic

Stress Disorder and Major Depressive Disorder. The psychologist also testified at her immigration court hearing, explaining the teenager's difficulties talking about what had happened to her. Nevertheless, the immigration judge denied the asylum claim based on the filing deadline, concluding that the teenager could have rectified her feelings of shame by seeking out an attorney. The BIA upheld the immigration judge's decision to deny asylum. The immigration court and the BIA also denied her asylum based on a purported lack of "nexus" between the persecution and a protected ground for asylum, but the U.S. Department of Justice subsequently stipulated, before the U.S. Court of Appeals for the Second Circuit, to a remand on all of these issues including the filing deadline denial. The case is still pending before the BIA.

- **The asylum request of a gay man who had been attacked and tortured in Peru was rejected based on the filing deadline.** The man was frequently harassed as a child because he was perceived as effeminate.[179] As an adult, he struggled with his sexual identity and lived in fear of being harassed and persecuted if he were viewed to be a gay man. At one point, he was attacked and tortured by a gang of men when they caught him coming out of a gay bar. The man did not report the incident to the police because he believed they would not protect him given their hostility to people who were gay. The man fled to the United States, where he continued to struggle with his sexuality. He eventually received treatment and medication for Post-Traumatic Stress Disorder. The man subsequently began to live openly as a gay man. He realized that given the torture he had suffered already in Peru, he could not safely return home. He applied for asylum three years after he entered the country. The asylum office found that the man's situation constituted an extraordinary circumstance, but that he had not applied within a reasonable time. It rejected his request for asylum based on the filing deadline, and referred his case into the removal process based on the deadline. Before the immigration court hearing

began, the DHS trial attorney told the man that he believed he was credible and offered to stipulate to a grant of withholding of removal. The asylum seeker accepted this offer because he was afraid that if the case went to trial and he was ultimately not granted asylum that he would have to return to Peru. As a result of this decision, the man was not granted asylum due to the filing deadline.

- **A man from Chile who had been attacked and beaten due to his sexual orientation was denied asylum because of the filing deadline.** The man fled to the United States after being detained, physically assaulted, and even stabbed because he is homosexual.[180] When he arrived in the United States, he did not speak English, did not know that his sexual orientation might form the basis for an asylum claim, and suffered from depression and Post-Traumatic Stress Disorder due to the past persecution that he had suffered. He learned eight years after his arrival in the United States that the brutal attacks that he has suffered in Chile and his fear of persecution might qualify him for asylum and shortly thereafter he filed an asylum application. The asylum office rejected his request for asylum based on the filing deadline and the case was referred into immigration court removal proceedings. More than two years later, an immigration judge granted him withholding of removal, finding that he is more likely than not going to suffer further persecution if returned to Chile, but denied him asylum based on the filing deadline.

C. Refugees Who Waited for Conditions to Improve Denied Asylum

Some refugees flee their countries after suffering persecution, but do not apply for asylum immediately in the hope that they will be able to return home safely in the future. They closely monitor the situation in their country. In some cases, a specific incident convinces them that safe return is impossible, so they finally do apply for asylum, but can then find themselves barred under the filing deadline. While the regulations state that changed circumstances include "changes in conditions in the applicant's country of nationality,"[181] when asylum applicants file because they learn of an increased danger to themselves personally – for example their family at home suffers increased harm – they are sometimes denied the exception. The adjudicator's rationale for the denial is that there are no changed circumstances: the applicant fled out of fear of persecution and continues to fear the same persecution. For example:

- **A Christian convert who was persecuted in India was denied asylum under the filing deadline.** An Indian man sought asylum due to persecution that he testified he suffered because he converted from Hinduism to Christianity.[182] He testified that in India he was attacked three times, his business was vandalized, and his life was regularly threatened. He fled to the United States, but waited to apply for asylum because he hoped conditions for Christians in India would improve. The convert testified that he ultimately applied for asylum after Hindus killed his father-in-law, mistaking his father-in-law for him. The BIA upheld the immigration judge's denial of asylum based on the deadline, stating that: "The respondent's explanation that he was ultimately motivated to apply for asylum after his father-in-law was mistaken for him and killed does not adequately explain why, given the respondent's description of his past mistreatment and the threats against him, he did not apply for asylum sooner." While the BIA recognized that the man was a genuine refugee who faced a clear probability of persecution, warranting the withholding of his

removal, he was denied asylum in the United States based on the filing deadline.

- **A credible asylum applicant was denied asylum based on filing deadline after waiting to see if conditions would improve so she could return home.** The Senegalese woman, profiled in Section I above, fled her country when her parents attempted to submit her to FGM and a forced marriage to a man 40 years her senior. She fled to the United States, but attempted for several years to change her parents' minds so she could safely return home. When she learned that her parents had forced her younger sister to undergo FGM, she realized that she could never return to Senegal. The immigration judge found the woman credible, but denied asylum because of the filing deadline, stating that her sister's experiences did not constitute a changed circumstance because she had originally fled Senegal out of fear of being subjected to FGM. The woman appealed the decision, but was eventually ordered removed.

- **Two brothers targeted for honor killings in Yemen held to face clear probability of persecution in Yemen, but denied asylum based on filing deadline.** Two Yemeni brothers who were members of a low class clan in Yemen sought asylum in the United States.[183] One of the brothers had secretly married the daughter of a powerful military officer in Yemen, after the general had refused to allow the marriage to the lower class clan member. The couple had met after the daughter's brother became friends with her future husband at a university where they all studied. The general threatened to kill the newlyweds, and shot his own son after the son informed him of the marriage. The general attempted to find the couple and ordered that the new husband's brother be detained. This brother was then brutally tortured at a police station, and detained for three months without charges. The two brothers and the general's daughter eventually fled to the United States. The brothers later applied for asylum, but their applications were denied by the immigration court based on the filing deadline.

The court concluded that the general's rejection of an offer of reconciliation, transmitted through the intercession of the Yemeni Foreign Minister, did not constitute a changed circumstance, and that the applications were not filed within a reasonable time after this event. The U.S. Court of Appeals for the Sixth Circuit, which concluded that it lacked jurisdiction to review the filing deadline determinations, did rule that the brothers faced a clear probability of persecution entitling them to withholding of removal.

D. Refugees Who Lack Knowledge of Asylum Law Denied Asylum

"The [Immigration Judge] also noted that the [refugee from Zimbabwe] had stated at the asylum office that he delayed filing his application because he did not know the asylum process. The IJ stated that such a lack of knowledge did not warrant a waiver of the filing deadline."

-U.S. Court of Appeals for the Third Circuit, which concludes it lacks jurisdiction to review filing deadline denial for refugee facing clear probability of persecution[184]

Many refugees are unfamiliar with U.S. immigration law and so may not know that they qualify for asylum or that there is a one-year deadline. This problem is exacerbated by the isolation that some refugees experience upon coming to the United States. Unable to speak English, and fearful of being returned to their home countries, many refugees remain secluded within their homes and local communities where information about asylum and the legal process may be incorrect, scarce, or simply non-existent. When asked about the injustice of denying asylum to refugees who did not know about the deadline, Representative Bill McCollum (R-Fla.), one of the key drafters of the initial filing deadline provision and its principal sponsor in the House of Representatives, said that the "Immigration Service would be required to tell people who came in that they could apply for asylum and . . . how long it would take."[185] (This kind of notice to people who come in to

the country was never enacted or codified.) Recognizing the difficulty that many refugees face after entering this country, the USCIS Asylum Officer Basic Training manual instructs that "extreme isolation within a refugee community, profound language barriers, or profound difficulties in cultural acclimatization" may constitute an extraordinary circumstance exception to the filing deadline. This language is not included in the regulations.

In practice, legitimate refugees and *bona fide* asylum seekers who do not speak English and lack knowledge about asylum have been found to be ineligible for an exception to the filing deadline and denied asylum. For example:

- **A student who was jailed by the Burmese military regime for his pro-democracy activities was denied asylum by the United States based on the filing deadline despite isolation and lack of English.** The Burmese student fled to the United States after being jailed for several years for his pro-democracy activities.[186] The student did not speak English, lived in isolation after his arrival, and did not learn about asylum until after he later met other Burmese refugees. The Immigration Court concluded that even if the student's extreme isolation constituted an exception to the filing deadline, he had not filed within a reasonable time. The student was denied asylum even though he was found to be credible and to face a clear probability of persecution, requiring the withholding of his removal. The U.S. Court of Appeals for the Sixth Circuit did not overturn the asylum denial.

- **An Ivorian pro-democracy activist who was enslaved and isolated after fleeing to the United States was denied asylum based on the filing deadline.** The woman and her fiancé were members of a political opposition party in Côte d'Ivoire.[187] Her fiancé, who was a leader in the party, was arrested by government militia because of his peaceful political activities, and was never seen again. When members of the militia continued to target the woman, she fled the country. She was able to make her way to the United States by agreeing to an arrangement that turned out to amount to indentured servitude. She was forced to live and work in a house as arranged by the man who helped her flee Côte d'Ivoire. She was extremely isolated. The woman was only able to apply for asylum more than a year later, after she escaped from the house. The asylum office rejected the woman's asylum application based on the filing deadline, and her case was put into the removal process. She is currently awaiting a hearing before the immigration court. The immigration judge has already expressed his view that it may be almost impossible for the woman to succeed in her asylum request given the filing deadline.

- **The asylum request of an advocate for women's rights was rejected based on the filing deadline despite her serious difficulties after arriving in the United States.** In Cameroon, an outspoken advocate for the rights of women, especially on issues relating to domestic violence, FGM, and reproductive health, worked for the United Nations and organized events to raise awareness.[188] She also spoke out against the corrupt practices of government officials. Because of her activism, the woman and her family were threatened and detained by a local tribal ruler, and their house was set on fire. She fled to the United States but was homeless for long periods of time, during which she slept on park benches and on church floors. After the woman found a steady place to live, she learned about asylum and applied soon thereafter without an attorney. The asylum officer who interviewed the woman told her that he believed her story, but he rejected her case based on the filing deadline after finding that she was not eligible for an exception. Her case was referred to the immigration court because of the filing deadline and is currently pending.

E. Refugees Who Lack Adequate Counsel Denied Asylum

Refugees often have difficulty finding affordable, trustworthy representation to help them with asylum applications. Many refugees lack information about the U.S. legal and immigration systems and do not understand how to file an asylum claim, which requires a particularly complex legal argument.[189] Two-thirds of asylum applicants are not represented at the asylum office level according to one study, and another study found that only 12 percent of unrepresented affirmative applicants are granted asylum, compared with 39 percent of applicants with representation.[190] According to a 2010 study by the Transactional Records Access Clearinghouse (TRAC) at Syracuse University, during fiscal year 2010, "only 11 percent of those without legal representation were granted asylum; with legal representation the odds rose to 54 percent."[191] Highly qualified representation can increase an applicant's probability of gaining asylum even more.[192] Indeed, another recent study conducted by legal experts found that having representation is "the single most important factor affecting the outcome of [an asylum] case."[193]

In many parts of the country, there is a dearth of low-cost or *pro bono* asylum attorneys, especially outside of urban centers.[194] Asylum seekers rely for the most part on nonprofit legal services agencies, which are typically under-resourced, so it can take many months before an asylum seeker can even get an appointment to be interviewed for potential legal representation.[195] Because asylum applications with filing deadline issues require additional resources to prepare, some organizations are not able to accept these cases at all. Human Rights First has interviewed many asylum seekers who were turned away by other nonprofit agencies because their cases involved filing deadline issues.

After trying in vain to find a qualified representative, many asylum seekers file without an attorney (*pro se*) in order to meet the deadline. The unfortunate result can be poorly prepared applications, sometimes with inconsistencies or missing details due to language issues or lack of understanding of complex U.S. government forms. The former director of a legal services organization in Colorado told a Human Rights First researcher that:

> We see many people who were denied at the asylum office after filing *pro se*. Their cases are very poorly prepared. When we ask them why they didn't go to a lawyer first, they tell us they had to rush to meet the deadline, and they could not find a lawyer in time.

> We had a woman from Sudan who filed one week before the deadline, fearing that she would miss the deadline. She only filled out the space available on the form, not realizing that she could attach additional information. When she got to the asylum office, she revealed new information during the interview, and the officer said her claim was inconsistent because she hadn't written it on the application form.[196]

Due to the shortage of reputable legal service organizations, many refugees turn to non-lawyers for assistance with their asylum applications. Sometimes well-meaning family members or friends provide advice; other times, refugees are taken advantage of by unscrupulous notarios who charge large fees without diligently preparing the asylum application.[197] By the time refugees learn that their applications have not been submitted properly – or at all – the filing deadline may have passed. Sometimes, refugees receive erroneous legal advice that they are not eligible to file for asylum because the deadline has already passed. The exceptions account for delay due to ineffective assistance of counsel, but the requirements to prove ineffective assistance are very complex[198] and only apply to assistance provided by attorneys and accredited representatives (non-lawyers who have been certified by the Department of Justice).[199] As a result, some adjudicators do not recognize that mistaken advice from others could potentially constitute the kind of circumstances that warrant an exception to the filing

deadline. (Human Rights First believes that the filing deadline's extraordinary circumstances exception could and should be applied in these circumstances.)

In reality, refugees whose late filing is the result of a lack of legal representation or the result of misadvice by others are often found to be ineligible for an exception and have been denied exceptions to the filing deadline. Examples include:

- **A nurse from Zimbabwe who was persecuted due to her peaceful political protest and labor rights advocacy had her asylum request rejected due to the filing deadline.** [200] The nurse from Zimbabwe, whose case was profiled in Section I of this report had her asylum case rejected based on the filing deadline after her original attorney failed to file her asylum application in time to meet her one year filing deadline. As detailed above, the nurse's case was referred into immigration court removal proceedings. She was ultimately granted withholding of removal, though she was not granted asylum.

- **A young Haitian girl was advised that she was too young to apply for asylum, then she was denied based on the filing deadline.** The 14-year old Haitian girl fled to the United States after a government-supported gang targeted and attacked her older brother, who was affiliated with an opposition political party.[201] After he fled the country, the gang returned to his house and threatened and beat his family members, including the young girl, to try to locate him. The girl's mother sent her to the United States to live with an uncle to avoid any more harm. The girl did not apply for asylum when she arrived due to severe PTSD and a lack of knowledge of asylum law. When she asked about applying for asylum, trusted family members and friends told her that she could not apply until she turned 21. Soon after she turned 21, in 2008, she submitted her asylum application. The asylum officer found that there were "extraordinary circumstances" that could exempt her from the filing deadline bar, but concluded that she did not file within a reasonable time of those circumstances. Her case was then referred to immigration court and her hearing is scheduled for late in 2011.

F. The "Reasonable Period" Hurdle: Exception Exists But Refugee's Late Filing Still Not Excused

Even refugees who can demonstrate "extraordinary" or "changed" circumstances are sometimes denied an exception to the filing deadline if adjudicators conclude that they did not file for asylum within "a reasonable period of time" after the circumstance that caused the delay. While this "reasonable period" requirement was added by the regulations, the regulations do not provide a definition of a "reasonable period."[202] The Asylum Officer Basic Training manual gives some guidance on this issue, explaining that it requires a fact-specific analysis and that "asylum officers should ask themselves if a reasonable person under the same or similar circumstances as the applicant would have filed sooner."[203] The manual also explains that "[a]n applicant's education and level of sophistication, the amount of time it takes to obtain legal assistance, any effects of persecution and/or illness, when the applicant became aware of the changed circumstance, and any other relevant factors should be considered."[204]

In our research, Human Rights First learned of many cases in which asylum seekers who have demonstrated eligibility for an exception were still denied asylum because the adjudicator did not find their filing dates to be "reasonable." Some examples include:

- **An asylum request rejected based on filing deadline because Colombian man applied six weeks after exception was triggered.** A man from Colombia fled to the United States and applied for asylum six weeks after his valid visa expired, but beyond the one-year filing deadline.[205] The asylum officer acknowledged that having a valid immigration

status was an extraordinary circumstance, but indicated that applying for asylum six weeks after the visa had expired was not reasonable. Yet the Asylum Officer Basic Training manual contains an example with similar facts that indicates that an eight-week period – two weeks longer than in the man's case – would ordinarily be considered reasonable.[206] After the asylum office rejected the man's asylum request based on the filing deadline, the man submitted a motion to reconsider in light of the manual's example, but the motion was denied.

- **A rape survivor's asylum request was initially rejected despite extraordinary circumstances relating to her serious medical conditions.** A woman with links to the political opposition in an African country was raped by government soldiers and contracted HIV as a result.[207] Following her arrival in the United States, the woman was hospitalized with AIDS and subsequently developed a nerve disorder which left her paralyzed and bedridden. For years, she remained unable to perform the most basic self-care. At the time of her asylum application, she continued to suffer from debilitating muscle weakness and was unable to walk without assistance. The asylum office found that the woman's poor health constituted an extraordinary circumstance justifying her delay but nevertheless determined that she had not filed within a reasonable time. The woman's asylum request was rejected based on the filing deadline, and her case was referred to immigration court. More than a year later, she was ultimately granted asylum.

- **A Gambian woman facing clear probability of persecution was denied an exception because she waited eight months after baby's birth to file for asylum.** A Gambian woman who had undergone FGM applied for asylum after her daughter was born in the United States because she wanted to protect her daughter from also being mutilated.[208] The immigration court acknowledged that the daughter's birth qualified as a changed circumstance, but did not grant an exception to the filing deadline because the woman had waited eight months after the birth to file. The court considered eight months to be unreasonable even though, during this time, the woman was recovering from labor and also had to take care of her son, who suffers from severe asthma and microcephaly. The BIA upheld the immigration judge's denial of asylum, but recognizing that the woman faced a clear probability of persecution, extended her withholding of removal.

- **The asylum request of a persecuted Zimbabwean pro-democracy advocate was rejected despite changed conditions.** A member of the major political opposition party in Zimbabwe, the Movement for Democratic Change (MDC), was repeatedly threatened and beaten by government officials.[209] He left for the United States on a student visa, planning to return to Zimbabwe when conditions improved. But as the human rights situation in Zimbabwe worsened in the months preceding national elections in 2008, the man decided to apply for asylum. The asylum office concluded that he had established changed circumstances materially affecting his eligibility for asylum. However, despite the dramatic changes occurring in Zimbabwe, his asylum request was rejected as untimely as the asylum office concluded that he had failed to file his application within a reasonable time period of those changes. His case was then put into the removal process and now remains pending before the immigration court.

The "changed circumstances" and "extraordinary circumstances" exceptions do not remedy the problems created by the filing deadline. Many legitimate refugees are still denied asylum, sometimes because adjudicators inappropriately deny them exceptions, sometimes because adjudicators decide that they did not file timely even given the exception, and sometimes because adjudicators decide the exceptions do not apply to the asylum seeker's circumstances. Not only do the exceptions fail to protect legitimate refugees with well-founded fears of persecution, but when exceptions are denied, their asylum cases are put into the immigration court removal process where they will consume additional government resources.

V. Lack of Judicial Review Increases Risk of Return to Persecution

"This Court has decided that this section divests us of jurisdiction to review decisions of whether an alien complied with the one-year time limit, or whether extraordinary circumstances were present to justify untimely filing of the asylum application."

- U.S. Court of Appeals for the Eleventh Circuit, in concluding that it lacked jurisdiction to review asylum denial for refugee facing clear probability of political persecution who filed 21 days late. [210]

The U.S. Courts of Appeals have played a crucial role in helping to ensure that immigration courts and the BIA do not mistakenly deport refugees in violation of U.S. law and this country's treaty commitments.[211] But when an asylum seeker is barred from asylum under the filing deadline, he or she cannot appeal that decision to most of the federal courts. The Illegal Immigration Reform and Immigrant Responsibility Act of 1996 included a provision that federal courts may not "review" claims related to the filing deadline.[212] Congress later restored partial judicial review through the REAL ID Act of 2005. As a result, the federal courts may consider "constitutional claims" and "questions of law" with respect to most jurisdictional bars to relief (including the filing deadline).[213] However, the circuits have split over whether they may consider a determination that an applicant does not qualify for an exception to the deadline as a "question of law," or whether it is instead an unreviewable factual question.[214]

Currently, only the Second and Ninth Circuits provide review of filing deadline decisions, and that review is limited to questions of law and constitutional claims.[215] As a result, if the BIA fails to correct a mistaken filing deadline denial for a refugee, that mistake cannot be reviewed and corrected in most parts of the country. As noted above, 19 percent of BIA asylum decisions in the period analyzed through the BIA Asylum Filing Deadline Analysis project included filing deadline issues.[216] Since the filing deadline went into effect, federal courts have declined to consider appeals of asylum filing deadline denials in many published and unpublished cases.[213] While there is no way to know how many deserving refugees were denied asylum or ordered deported due to the lack of federal court review of filing deadline denials in so many federal circuit courts, it is clear that the Board has denied asylum – based on the filing deadline – in a significant number of cases in which federal court review might have changed the result. For example:

- **A woman who fled forced abortion was found to face clear probability of persecution in China, but federal court held it does not have jurisdiction to review denial of asylum based on filing deadline.** A pregnant Chinese woman who feared that she would be persecuted and subjected to a forced abortion in China fled to the United States, where she gave birth to a daughter.[217] She obtained a work visa and remained employed for several years. Six and a half months after her work visa expired, she applied for asylum. She was denied asylum based on the filing deadline because the immigration judge did not find the six-month period between the time her visa expired, and her date of filing for asylum, to be "reasonable." The U.S. Court of Appeals for the Fifth Circuit concluded that the woman faced a clear probability of persecution, entitling her to withholding of removal. But the Fifth Circuit did not even consider the woman's asylum claim because it ruled that it did not have jurisdiction to review the filing deadline determination.

- **A victim of terrorist kidnapping and persecution was found to face clear probability of persecution in Colombia, but federal court concluded it could not review denial of asylum based on filing deadline.** An active member of a political party was persecuted by the Revolutionary Armed Forces of Colombia (FARC).[218] Because of his peaceful political activities, the FARC repeatedly threatened him. FARC members killed or kidnapped his companions and threatened to kill the man if he did not end his political work. When he started receiving threatening phone calls at his house, the man went into hiding. The FARC found him and kidnapped him, beating him and holding him for more than two weeks. The man fled to the United States days after he escaped. The immigration court concluded that his asylum request was barred because he filed 21 days after his filing deadline passed. The immigration judge and the BIA also denied him withholding of removal. While the U.S. Court of Appeals for the Eleventh Circuit concluded that he faced a clear probability of persecution in Colombia, and therefore found the man eligible for withholding of removal, the court held that it lacked jurisdiction to review the filing deadline determination. As a result, the court did not overturn the denial of asylum.

Moreover, when federal court review of filing deadline denials does exist, the federal courts have been able to correct mistaken applications of the filing deadline and help protect legitimate refugees and *bona fide* asylum seekers from asylum denials and deportation to persecution. For example:

- **An Iranian woman who faced clear probability of persecution due to her conversion to Christianity was initially denied asylum based on the filing deadline, but federal court overturned mistaken filing deadline determination.** The Iranian Muslim woman came to the United States as a tourist.[219] Many years later, while still in the United States, she began attending a Christian church and volunteered in the church's nursery. She testified that she was very attracted to Christianity's focus on forgiveness and kindness, and eventually converted. Fearing that she would be persecuted if she returned to Iran and continued observing Christianity, she applied for asylum seven months after her conversion. In her testimony, the woman explained that she waited to apply because she wanted to ensure that her new faith would be a lifelong commitment. Her pastor supported her application and testified at her immigration court hearing. The woman also submitted a petition signed by 91 parishioners attesting to her dedication to the church. The immigration judge found the woman to be a refugee, and granted her withholding of removal, but denied her request for asylum based on the filing deadline. He found that the woman's conversion was a changed circumstance, but that waiting seven months after her conversion to apply for asylum was not a reasonable delay. The BIA affirmed the decision. The woman then filed a petition for review to the U.S. Court of Appeals for the Ninth Circuit. The court ruled that the immigration judge's filing deadline decision was not supported by substantial evidence. The court concluded that the woman had offered substantial evidence that her conversion was a process that began on the date of her conversion ceremony but took time to incorporate into her life and that she had applied for asylum within a reasonable period after her conversion. The court then remanded the case back to the BIA, noting that she satisfied the asylum standard, in order to determine whether to exercise its discretion to grant her asylum.

- **A Chinese pro-democracy activist was denied asylum based on the filing deadline, but a federal court ruled that the denial was legal error.** The Chinese man applied for asylum several years after arriving in the United States, and five months after discovering that the Chinese government had learned of his work with the opposition China Democratic Party (CDP).[220] The man attended rallies, wrote articles, and recruited CDP members within China over the telephone. The U.S. Court of

Appeals noted that the genuineness of the man's political activity with the CDP was not questioned by the U.S. government. The immigration court found that the man's application for asylum was not timely, and concluded that he was not eligible for an exception. The court denied him both asylum and withholding, and the Board upheld the denials. The U.S. Court of Appeals for the Second Circuit, after explaining that it had jurisdiction to review questions of law concerning a filing deadline exception, ruled that the BIA made a legal error in its decision to deny a deadline exception in this case. The Court also remanded the case on the merits, explaining that an asylum seeker can indeed demonstrate a well-founded fear of persecution when his involvement with a banned group may become known after his return.

Conclusion and Recommendation

The only effective and comprehensive remedy to the problems outlined in this report is to eliminate the filing deadline altogether. As long as there is a deadline – even if the time period were significantly extended – genuine refugees will continue to be denied asylum on the basis of a technicality, and significant resources will be expended throughout the adjudication system to apply this procedural hurdle. Eliminating the deadline will improve the efficiency and effectiveness of the immigration adjudication system by allowing adjudicators to save time and resources – or reallocate them to address the merits of cases – rather than expending significant time and resources assessing a technical filing requirement. This reform would also help to reduce the number of cases referred into the already overburdened and backlogged immigration court system. Finally, as detailed in this report, many measures are in place to actually combat abuse in the immigration system.

As this report has shown, the filing deadline prevents genuine refugees from obtaining asylum in contravention of U.S. commitments to protect refugees who have fled persecution and despite Congressional intent to provide protection to legitimate asylum applicants. The deadline is inefficient, unnecessary, and diverts time from adjudication of the merits of the asylum claim itself. For these reasons, Human Rights First calls upon Congress to eliminate the one-year filing deadline for asylum claims as soon as possible.

Appendix:
Survey of Human Rights First *Pro Bono* Filing Deadline Cases

As part of Human Rights First's research into the impact of the asylum filing deadline on refugees who seek asylum in the United States, we reviewed 401 asylum cases – all of the new *pro bono* cases that were taken on for legal representation in our *pro bono* program during the four-year period from 2005 through 2008.

Through its *pro bono* Asylum Legal Representation Program, Human Rights First identifies refugees in need of legal representation and recruits volunteer attorneys to represent them in connection with their applications for asylum in the United States. Prior to placement, Human Rights First conducts an extensive interview with the asylum seeker to determine whether he or she is a *bona fide* refugee. We then work closely with the volunteer attorneys, providing legal support and advice throughout the case. More than 90 percent of our clients ultimately win relief in their cases.

The findings of this survey, as detailed below, illustrate the impact of the filing deadline on refugees in various ways, including:

- **The filing deadline impacts genuine refugees.** While all asylum cases involve an examination of the filing deadline, 20 percent of Human Rights First's cases during the four-year period involved applications that were filed more than one year after the asylum seeker's arrival in the United States or were rejected by the asylum office based on the filing deadline and were referred into immigration court removal proceedings. The overwhelming majority of these individuals were ultimately recognized to be refugees by U.S. adjudicators, confirming that they were indeed refugees entitled to protection despite their late filing or other filing deadline complications.

- **The asylum cases of many refugees could be resolved more efficiently if there were no filing deadline.** Of the Human Rights First cases that were rejected by the asylum office based on the filing deadline, 75 percent were subsequently granted asylum or withholding of removal (as a result of the filing deadline) and 17 percent are still pending in immigration court. As detailed below, this grant rate will likely increase as the pending cases are resolved. This means that nearly all of these cases could have been resolved more quickly and without the need for immigration court removal proceedings if there were no filing deadline.

- **Genuine refugees sometimes require more than a year to file for asylum.** Of Human Rights First's successful late-filing refugee clients, 63 percent filed more than two years after arrival, 45 percent filed more than three years after arrival, and 20 percent filed more than five years after arrival. All of these individuals were genuine refugees, as confirmed by their subsequent grants of asylum or other protection by U.S. adjudicators.

- **The filing deadline delays the successful resolution of asylum cases.** Once Human Rights First's filing deadline cases were rejected at the asylum office based on the filing deadline, they took much longer to resolve: While two-thirds of asylum office grants occurred within six months, in immigration court only 15 percent of asylum grants occurred within one year. In fact, one-third of these cases took more than two years to resolve, and 15 percent took more than three years.

- **Women refugees who are affected by the filing deadline are not granted asylum, and are instead**

given only withholding of removal, in a higher percentage of cases. While 90 percent of male filing deadline applicants were granted asylum, only 63 percent of female filing deadline applicants were granted asylum. Similarly, only 2 percent of male filing deadline applicants were granted withholding of removal, while 13 percent of female filing deadline applicants were granted withholding of removal. This divergence is not present among Human Rights First's non-filing deadline cases, where both male and female applicants were granted asylum and withholding of removal at the same rates.

While Human Rights First's *pro bono* cases are not necessarily representative of the entire asylum-seeking population, this survey does make clear that many legitimate refugees are being delayed and often denied asylum as a result of the filing deadline.

A. The Filing Deadline and Human Rights First's Cases

From 2005 to 2008, Human Rights First took on for representation through its *pro bono* program the cases of 401 asylum seekers after conducting interviews and assessments to determine that the individuals were indeed refugees within the meaning of the Refugee Convention and Protocol. (During this time period, Human Rights First's overall case load ranged from 1,100 to 1,200 open cases, most of which had been accepted into our program in prior years.)

While compliance with the filing deadline had to be addressed in all of these cases, 79 of these 401 new cases – or 20 percent – had significant filing deadline issues. These cases were considered "filing deadline cases" by Human Rights First if the applicant applied for asylum more than one year after entering the United States, or if the asylum office had rejected the applicant based on the filing deadline and referred the case to immigration court. 62 of the 401 new Human Rights First

cases were for asylum seekers who had gone through the expedited removal process. Because expedited removal applicants are apprehended upon or soon after entering the United States and placed directly into immigration court proceedings, their cases are much less likely to trigger the one-year filing deadline. Removing these clients from the total caseload raises the percentage of filing deadline cases to 23 percent - nearly one-fourth of Human Rights First's non-expedited removal caseload.

Additionally, Human Rights First accepted 54 cases where the applicant had not filed for asylum and the filing deadline was less than four months – and in some cases less than one month – from the time the case was accepted. In these cases, asylum seekers were able to file timely due to the assistance of Human Rights First *pro bono* attorneys or Human Rights First staff attorneys. Without this legal assistance – often under extremely short deadlines – these asylum seekers may have also run afoul of the filing deadline, thereby imperiling their chances of obtaining asylum.

B. Time to Apply for Asylum

There are two main ways an asylum seeker can run afoul of the filing deadline. First, he or she may apply for asylum more than one year after arriving in the United States. As discussed in the accompanying report, there are many reasons why *bona fide* refugees are not able to apply within one year. Second, even refugees who do file within a year of their arrival can run afoul of the deadline, if an adjudicator decides that the refugee cannot prove date of entry into the United States and as a result concludes (mistakenly or not) that the refugee cannot show that the application was timely filed. Human Rights First's filing deadline cases reflect both of these scenarios.

As noted above, 20 percent of Human Rights First's cases during the four-year period involved applications that were filed more than one year after the asylum seeker's arrival in the United States or were rejected by the asylum office based on the filing deadline and were referred into immigration court removal proceedings. 17 percent of Human Rights First's cases during the four-year period involved applications that were filed more than one year after the asylum seeker's arrival in the United States and are still pending in the immigration courts.

The chart below shows the time it took for Human Rights First's refugee clients to file for asylum in the 68 filing deadline cases that were eventually granted relief (ie, confirming that U.S. adjudicators concluded that these were bona fide refugees). Some of these applicants were granted asylum by the asylum office, others were granted asylum in immigration court after having been referred, and some were not granted an exception but were only extended withholding of removal.

TIME FOR SUCCESSFUL HRF REFUGEE FILING DEADLINE CASES TO APPLY FOR ASYLUM

MONTHS AFTER ARRIVAL	NUMBER OF CASES	PERCENT OF SUCCESSFUL FILING DEADLINE CASES	PERCENT OF SUCCESSFUL LATE FILERS
12-23	22	32%	37%
24-35	11	16%	18%
36-47	9	13%	15%
48-59	6	9%	10%
60-71	8	12%	13%
72-83	3	5%	5%
84-95	0	0%	0%
96-107	1	1%	2%
Timely filed but could not show date of entrance	8	12%	N/A

This chart makes clear that even if the filing deadline were extended for an additional year, it would continue to bar legitimate refugees from asylum. Extending the filing deadline to two years would still have affected two-thirds of our successful filing deadline cases; extending it to three years would still have affected half. A longer filing deadline – no matter its length – would not have exempted the 12 percent of genuine refugees who were considered to not have sufficient proof of their date of entrance. And of course any filing deadline would lead to the inefficiencies and diversion of resources discussed below and in the accompanying report.

C. Adjudication Resources and Time

A review of Human Rights First's filing deadline cases also demonstrates the additional governmental resources and time that are expended in resolving many filing deadline cases. In fact, as illustrated by Human Rights First's filing deadline cases, it takes much longer for filing deadline cases to be resolved after they are rejected at the initial asylum office level based on the filing deadline and referred into removal proceedings.

30 of the Human Rights First filing deadline cases

included in this study were granted asylum by the asylum office. All of these cases required only one interview with an asylum officer, usually lasting less than four hours. In contrast, 26 of our filing deadline cases were originally interviewed at the asylum office, but rejected based on the filing deadline and eventually granted asylum or withholding in immigration court. In addition to the original asylum office interview, all of these cases had at least two hearing dates – one brief master calendar hearing and one intensive individual merits hearing. In fact, ten cases, or 38 percent, required three or more appearances before a decision was granted. Nine out of ten of these cases required at least two individual merits hearing dates, and four out of ten required at least three. As detailed in the accompanying report, these hearings required the time of at least three government employees - the immigration judge, a government trial attorney and a court clerk.

Once these cases were referred to the immigration courts, they took much longer to resolve. The significant delays in the immigration courts have been documented repeatedly,[*] and as detailed in the accompanying report, addressing issues relating to the asylum filing deadline can also add some time and divert resources before the immigration courts. Asylum cases can spend years on an immigration court's docket, resulting in hardship for asylum applicants and their families. To illustrate the additional time and resources expended to resolve a filing deadline case after it is rejected at the asylum office based on the filing deadline, we have compared the amount of time it took to resolve our filing deadline cases at the asylum office and the immigration court levels, respectively.

TOTAL ADJUDICATION TIME FOR APPLICANTS GRANTED ASYLUM AT THE ASYLUM OFFICE

MONTHS AFTER APPLYING	NUMBER OF CASES	PERCENT OF TOTAL
2 or less	5	16%
3	8	27%
4	3	10%
5	2	7%
6	2	7%
7	2	7%
8	0	0%
9	1	3%
10	2	7%
More than 12	5	16%

This data shows that almost half of Human Rights First's successful filing deadline cases were granted asylum by the asylum office within three months of applying. Two-thirds were granted within six months. Only 16 percent of HRF's clients in successful filing deadline cases waited more than a year to be granted asylum.

Contrast these statistics with the adjudication time for refugees referred by the asylum office on the filing deadline and eventually granted asylum or withholding in immigration court. All or nearly all of these refugees could have been granted at the asylum office but for the filing deadline.

* See, e.g., AMERICAN BAR ASSOCIATION COMMISSION ON IMMIGRATION: REFORMING THE IMMIGRATION SYSTEM: EXECUTIVE SUMMARY (2010), http://new. abanet.org/Immigration/Documents/ReformingtheImmigrationSystemExecutiveSummary.pdf; TRAC IMMIGRATION, IMMIGRATION COURTS: STILL A TROUBLED INSTITUTION (June 30, 2009), http://trac.syr.edu/immigration/reports/210/; APPLESEED, ASSEMBLY LINE INJUSTICE: BLUEPRINT TO REFORM AMERICA'S IMMIGRATION COURTS 10-11 (May 2009), http://appleseeds.net/Portals/0/Documents/Publications/Assembly%20Line%20Injustice.pdf.

TOTAL ADJUDICATION TIME FOR APPLICANTS REFERRED BY ASYLUM OFFICE AND GRANTED ASYLUM OR WITHHOLDING IN IMMIGRATION COURT

MONTHS AFTER APPLYING	NUMBER OF CASES	PERCENT OF TOTAL
Less than 12	4	15%
13-18	6	23%
19-24	7	27%
25-30	4	15%
31-36	1	4%
37-42	1	4%
43-48	0	0%
49-54	3	12%

Here, the statistics are essentially switched. Whereas only 16 percent of asylum office grants required *more than* one year, in immigration court only 15 percent of asylum grants occur *within* one year. In fact, one-third of these cases took more than two years, and 15 percent took more than three years.

The wait times become even more extreme for recent cases due to the current backlog in immigration courts. Human Rights First had 6 asylum cases that were referred from the asylum office on the filing deadline that were still in proceedings at the time of publication. Four of these continuing cases will require more than two years before they are adjudicated. Three will require more than three years.

The longer it takes to resolve a case, the more government time and resources are expended. Given that the majority of these asylum applicants are ultimately found to be genuine refugees, the deadline leads to a needless waste of limited resources.

D. Outcome of Filing Deadline Cases

Of our 79 filing deadline clients, 86 percent were eventually granted asylum or withholding of removal – confirming that they were indeed refugees with legitimate asylum claims. 14 percent of the 79 are still pending. (Human Rights First's overall success rate in asylum cases exceeds 90 percent This rate significantly exceeds

the national asylum grant rate for several reasons: Human Rights First conducts extensive assessments to determine if an individual is a refugee before taking on a case; its clients are represented by counsel while some asylum seekers are not able to obtain legal representation; its *pro bono* lawyers provide excellent legal representation; and the cases are also supported by Human Rights First's legal expertise on a wide range of asylum issues, including the filing deadline.)

6 percent of our filing deadline clients were not granted asylum but did receive withholding of removal. However, as detailed in the body of the accompanying report, withholding of removal provides refugees with only limited protection from deportation, and does not permit them to bring their children or spouses to safety in the United States as derivative asylees. Their ability to integrate is undermined by their lack of a stable status. They cannot apply for legal residence as can asylees, leaving them in long-term limbo.

Additionally, more than half of the withholding of removal grants were the result of a "settlement" offered by the DHS trial attorney. In such settlements, the Department of Homeland Security trial attorney offers the applicant withholding of removal in exchange for withdrawing his or her asylum application prior to the hearing. The applicant must decide whether to take a chance on receiving no relief and being ordered removed to the country where they fear persecution, or to settle for the limited relief of withholding. Sometimes the government trial attorney will pressure the applicant to accept the settlement by promising to appeal the immigration judge's decision if it is a favorable one, if the asylum seeker does not agree to the "offer" of withholding.

With respect to the success rate of HRF cases, we do not believe that these numbers are reflective of the larger asylum seeker population (for the reasons discussed above), and we would expect that asylum grant rates would be much lower for the broader filing deadline population. Many legitimate refugees – including those who are not able to obtain representation – are certainly denied asylum or other protection as a result of the filing deadline, as detailed in the accompanying report. However, as noted above, the success rate in Human Rights First's filing deadline cases does demonstrate that this pool of cases were overwhelmingly recognized as "refugees" by U.S. government adjudicators – and thus illustrates the impact of the filing deadline on some refugees who have been through – or are still in – the U.S. asylum and immigration adjudication system.

OUTCOME OF HRF FILING DEADLINE CASES

OUTCOME	NUMBER OF CASES	PERCENT OF FILING DEADLINE CASES
Asylum	63	80%
Withholding through IJ decision	2	2%
Withholding through settlement	3	4%
No relief granted (but appeals pending at BIA/federal courts)	4	5%
No decision yet (pending at immigration court)	7	9%

However, to understand the impact of the filing deadline on refugees, it is necessary to disaggregate the data by what happened at each level of adjudication.

Of its larger number of filing deadline cases, Human Rights First accepted 35 filing deadline cases (44 percent of total filing deadline cases) at the asylum office stage. Human Rights First accepted the remaining 44 filing deadline cases (56 percent of total filing deadline cases) at the defensive stage, when the application is adjudicated in immigration court. Of the defensive cases, 31 had been referred by the asylum office because of the filing deadline prior to Human Rights First's accepting the case. Eight had been referred for reasons other than the filing deadline. Even though an exception to the filing deadline had presumably been granted in these cases, the clients still had to address the filing deadline again in immigration court. Finally, five defensive cases were placed in immigration court proceedings after the asylum seeker had been apprehended by DHS. Those asylum applications did not start at the asylum office, but rather were adjudicated solely in immigration court.

OUTCOME OF CASES ACCEPTED AT ASYLUM OFFICE

OUTCOME	NUMBER OF CASES	PERCENT OF TOTAL
Asylum granted by asylum office	30	86%
Referred on filing deadline but granted asylum by immigration court	3	8%
Referred on filing deadline and still pending at immigration court	1	3%
Denied for reasons other than the filing deadline	1	3%

OUTCOME OF CASES ACCEPTED AT IMMIGRATION COURT
AFTER BEING REFERRED ON FILING DEADLINE

OUTCOME	NUMBER OF CASES	PERCENT OF TOTAL
Asylum	19	62%
Withholding through IJ decision	2	6%
Withholding through settlement	2	6%
No relief granted (but appeals pending at BIA/federal courts)	3	10%
No decision yet (pending at immigration court)	5	16%

OUTCOME OF CASES ACCEPTED AT IMMIGRATION COURT
AFTER BEING REFERRED FOR OTHER REASONS

OUTCOME	NUMBER OF CASES	PERCENT OF TOTAL
Asylum	8	100%

OUTCOME OF CASES ACCEPTED AT IMMIGRATION COURT
AFTER BEING APPREHENDED BY DHS

OUTCOME	NUMBER OF CASES	PERCENT OF TOTAL
Asylum	3	60%
Withholding through settlement	1	20%
No decision yet (pending at immigration court)	1	20%

Human Rights First draws several conclusions from this data:

- The cases of legitimate refugees are being rejected at the asylum office as a result of the asylum filing deadline. Between 2005 and 2008, Human Rights First represented 26 asylum seekers whose cases were rejected by the asylum office based on the filing deadline but were ultimately determined to be refugees entitled to protection.

- Of the Human Rights First cases that were rejected by the asylum office based on the filing deadline, 75 percent were subsequently granted asylum or withholding of removal (as a result of the filing deadline) while 17 percent are still pending in immigration court. This means that nearly all of these cases were put into the removal process, and therefore required immigration court hearings, even though these individuals were ultimately recognized to be refugees entitled to protection.[*]

G. Gender Breakdown

Within the filing deadline cases, 48 applicants, or 61 percent were male, 30 applicants, or 38 percent were female, and 1 applicant was transgender. This breakdown is roughly the same as our non-filing deadline cases, where 63 percent were male, 36 perent were female, and 1 percent were transgender.

However, while 90 percent of male filing deadline applicants were granted asylum, only 63 percent of female filing deadline applicants were granted asylum. Similarly, only 2 percent of male filing deadline applicants were granted withholding of removal, while 13 percent of female filing deadline applicants were granted withholding of removal. This disparity is not present among our non-filing deadline cases, where male and female applicants were granted asylum and withholding of removal at the same rates.

[*] The asylum office is not authorized to grant withholding of removal, but as these individuals were rejected by the office based only the filing deadline and were extended withholding of removal by the immigration court due to the deadline, these individuals would most likely have been able to be granted asylum at the asylum office but for the filing deadline.

Endnotes

1 While the filing deadline was passed in 1996, and went into effect in 1997, it did not begin to operate as a bar and impact newly filed cases until 1998.

2 President Barack Obama, Presidential Proclamation – World Refugee Day (June 20, 2010).

3 *See, e.g.,* UN Ad Hoc Committee on Refugees and Stateless Persons, *Report of the Ad Hoc Committee on Refugees and Stateless Persons, Second Session, Geneva 14 August to 25 August 1950,* U.N. Doc. E/AC.32/8;E/1850 (1950).

4 The U.S. acceded to the Protocol in 1968, thereby binding itself to the Refugee Convention. 1951 United Nations Convention Relating to the Status of Refugees, July 28, 1951, 19 U.S.T. 6259, 189 U.N.T.S. 150; 1967 United Nations Protocol Relating to the Status of Refugees, Jan. 31, 1967, 19 U.S.T. 6223, 606 U.N.T.S. 267.

5 The Refugee Act of 1980, Pub. L. 96-212, tit. I, 101(b), 94 Stat. 102 (1980). *See* Deborah E. Anker & Michael H. Posner, *The Forty Year Crisis: Legislative History of the Refugee Act of 1980,* 19 San Diego L. Rev. 9 (1981).

6 U.S. Dept. of Homeland Security, Refugees and Asylees: 2009 1 (2010), *available at* http://www.dhs.gov/xlibrary/assets/statistics/publications/ois_rfa_fr_2009.pdf.

7 U.S. Dept. of Homeland Security, 2009 Yearbook of Immigration Statistics tbl 13 (2010), *available at* http://www.dhs.gov/files/statistics/publications/YrBk09RA.shtm.

8 Comments of U.S. Secretary of State Hillary Clinton on June 18, 2010 in commemoration of World Refugee Day. See also UNHCR, Total Contributions to UNHCR in 2009, *available at* http://www.unhcr.org/pages/49c3646c26c.html.

9 INA § 208(a)(2)(D).

10 142 CONG. REC. S11840 (daily ed. Sept. 30, 1996) (statement of Sen. Hatch). See also Philip G. Schrag & Michele R. Pistone, *The New Asylum Rule: Not Yet a Model of Fair Procedure,* 11 Geo. Immigr. L.J. 267, 269 (1997).

11 *Supra* note 10 (statement of Sen. Hatch); see also 142 Cong. Rec. S4468 (daily ed. May 1996) (statement of Sen. Simpson that "[w]e are not after the person from Iraq, or the Kurd, or those people. We are after the people gimmicking the system."); Karen Musalo & Marcelle Rice, *Center for Gender and Refugee Studies: The Implementation of the One-Year Bar to Asylum,* 31 Hastings Int'l & Comp. L. Rev. 693 (2008); Michele R. Pistone & Philip G. Schrag, *The New Asylum Rule: Improved But Still Unfair,* 16 Geo. Immigr. L.J. 1, 10 (2001).

12 *See* Michele R. Pistone, Cato Inst., New Asylum Laws: Undermining an American Ideal 12 (1998), *available at* http://www.cato.org/pubs/pas/pa299.pdf; Leena Khandwala et al., *The One-Year Bar: Denying Protection to Bona Fide Refugees, Contrary to Congressional Intent and Violative of International Law,* 05-08 Immigr. Briefings 1 (Aug. 2005).

13 *See An Overview of Asylum Policy, Before the Subcomm. on Immigration of the Senate Comm. on the Judiciary,* 107th Congr. 45 (2001) (statement of Allen Keller, M.D., Founder and Director of the Bellevue/NYU School of Medicine Program for Survivors of Torture); see also Musalo & Rice supra note 11; Pistone *supra* note 12 at 12-14.

14 Lawyers Committee for Human Rights (now human rights first), Refugee Women at Risk: Unfair U.S. Laws Hurt Asylum Seekers 19 n. 7 (2002) [*hereinafter HRF Report Women at Risk*] available at http://www.humanrightsfirst.org/refugees/reports/refugee_women.pdf.

15 Lawyers Committee for Human Rights, Asylum Project: Summary of Statistical Review of 200 Randomly Selected Files of Asylum Clients (1996) (*cited with approval in* Pistone, *New Asylum Laws*).

16 *Soe v. Gonzales,* 227 Fed. Appx. 468 (6th Cir. 2007).

17 Case materials on file with Human Rights First; the information in this profile was provided by the asylum seeker's current attorney, Jonathan Nelson, Esq.

18 *See* Matter of Anon. (A# redacted) (BIA, Jan. 3, 2008) (on file with Human Rights First), obtained through Freedom of Information Act (FOIA) request filed by the National Immigrant Justice Center.

19 Filing deadline data provided by the USCIS Asylum Division on Dec. 16, 2009 as follow up to the Dec. 8, 2010 meeting. The U.S. Asylum Office and other statistical studies have however separated out these cases in their filing deadline analysis because, "[a]ccording to the Asylum Office, Mexicans voluntarily entered the affirmative asylum system in large numbers during this period principally in order to be placed into immigration court proceedings where they could seek relief other than asylum." Jaya Ramji-Nogales, Andrew I. Schoenholtz and Philip G. Schrag, Refugee Roulette: Disparities in Asylum Adjudication and Proposals for Reform (NYU Press 2009) p. 31, n. 7 [hereinafter Refugee Roulette].

20 *Id.*

21 FOIA response letter from Crystal Souza, Paralegal Specialist, U.S. Department of Justice Executive Office for Immigration Review to National Immigrant Justice Center (January 9, 2009) (on file with National Immigrant Justice Center).

22 NATIONAL IMMIGRANT JUSTICE CENTER, HUMAN RIGHTS FIRST & PENNSYLVANIA STATE UNIVERSITY DICKINSON SCHOOL OF LAW'S CENTER FOR IMMIGRANTS' RIGHTS, THE ONE-YEAR ASYLUM DEADLINE AND THE BIA: NO PROTECTION, NO PROCESS - AN ANALYSIS OF BOARD OF IMMIGRATION APPEALS, DECISIONS 2005 – 2008 (Sept. 2010) [*hereinafter* BIA Filing Deadline Case Analysis].

23 Survey of Human Rights First *Pro Bono* Filing Deadline Cases, Appendix 1, [hereinafter HRF 2010 Pro Bono Survey]. More information about Human Rights First's filing deadline cases can be found in the Appendix.

24 *Id.*

25 HRF case 68492. Represented by *pro bono* counsel at Pepper Hamilton LLP through the Human Rights First Asylum Legal Representation Program.

26 HRF case 96369. Represented by *pro bono* counsel at Clifford Chance LLP through the Human Rights First Asylum Legal Representation Program.

27 HRF case 72102. Represented by *pro bono* counsel at Milbank, Tweed, Hadley & McCloy LLP through the Human Rights First Asylum Legal Representation Program.

28 INA § 241(b)(3); *see e.g. INS v. Cardoza-Fonseca*, 480 U.S. 421, 423-24 (1987); *INS v. Stevic*, 467 U.S. 407, 416 (1984).

29 *Id.*

30 *See* EOIR, Fact Sheet: Asylum and Withholding of Removal Relief, Convention Against Torture Protections 6 (Jan. 15, 2009), *available at* http://www.aila.org/content/default.aspx?docid=27724.

31 *See, e.g., Kedjouti v. Holder*, 571 F.3d 718, 721 (7th Cir. 2009); *Gomis v. Holder*, 571 F.3d 353, 360 (4th Cir. 2009).

32 *Kang v. Attorney General*, No. 08-4790 (3d Cir. filed Jul. 8, 2010).

33 *See Gomis v. Holder*, 571 F.3d 353 (4th Cir. 2009); Petition for Writ of Certiorari for Petitioner, *Gomis v. Holder*, 175 L. Ed. 2d. 881 (2010), *available at* http://www.aclu.org/files/assets/2009-8-11-GomisvHolder-CertPetition.pdf

34 *Id.*

35 *Gomis,* 571 F.3d at 360.

36 *Id.* at 362.

37 *See* Matter of Anon. (A# redacted) (BIA, Jan. 16, 2008) (on file with Human Rights First), obtained through Freedom of Information Act (FOIA) request filed by the National Immigrant Justice Center.

38 *See Kedjouti v. Holder,* 571 F.3d 718 (7th Cir. 2009).

39 *Id.* at 721.

40 1951 UN Convention Relating to the Status of Refugees arts. 33-34, July 28, 1951, 189 U.N.T.S. 150. *See also* Protocol Relating to Status of Refugees, Jan. 31, 1967, 606 U.N.T.S. 267. The United States signed on to the Protocol in 1968, and by doing so bound itself to comply with the substantive obligations of the Refugee Convention.

41 UNHCR Exec. Comm., *Refugees Without an Asylum Country, Conclusion No. 15* (XXX), ¶ I (Oct. 16, 1979), *available at* http://www.unhcr.org/cgi-bin/texis/vtx/refworld/rwmain?docid=3ae68c960.

42 António Guterres, U.N. High Commissioner for Refugees, Closing Keynote at "Renewing U.S. Commitment to Refugee Protection: The 30th Anniversary of the Refugee Act," co-hosted by Human Rights First and Georgetown University Law Center in Washington, DC (Mar. 16, 2010).

43 INA § 208(a)(2)(B); 8 C.F.R. § 208.4(a)(2)(i)(A).

44 Asylum officers are instructed to apply the "clear and convincing" standard to both these dates. Compliance with the deadline can also be established by clear and convincing evidence that the applicant was outside the U.S. during the year immediately before the date of filing. See USCIS, Asylum Officer Basic Training Course: One-Year Filing Deadline 6-7 (Mar. 23, 2009) [hereinafter One-Year Deadline Training]; *see e.g. Khunaverdiants v. Mukasey,* 548 F.3d 760, 765-66 (9th Cir. 2008) (finding BIA erred in holding that proof of exact departure date was necessary to establish that applicant filed within one year because other clear and convincing evidence, specifically that the applicant was outside the country one year before filing, established that the application was filed within one year).

45 Human Rights First interview with Michele McKenzie, Advocates for Human Rights (May 12, 2010).

46 Human Rights First interview with Helen Harnett, National Immigrant Justice Center (Apr. 5, 2010).

47 HRF case 9568. Represented by pro bono counsel at White & Case LLP through the Human Rights First Asylum Legal Representation Program. The family's story was also profiled in *The New York Daily News.* Eric Herman, *Immigration: No Kid Glove,* NY Daily News, (Apr. 30, 2000); *An Overview of Asylum Policy Before the Subcomm. On Immigration of the Senate Comm. on the* Judiciary 107th Cong. 53 (2001) (statement of Makani Jalloh, asylee from Sierra Leone).

48 Celia W. Dugger, *Immigration Bills' Deadlines May Imperil Asylum Seekers,* N.Y. Times, Feb. 12, 1996, at B1.

49 Human Rights First interviews with Linette Tobin, Esq. Immigration Law Office of Linette Tobin (May 14, 2009 and August 16, 2010), Human Rights First interview with "Dehab" (May 14, 2009). For reasons of confidentiality, the refugee's real name has not been used in this profile.

50 Human Rights First interview of June 25, 2009 with Shoshanna Malett, Esq., who served as an Asylum Officer in New York from 1997 to 2006.

51 INA § 208(a)(2)(B).

52 *Supra* note 48.

53 Filing deadline data provided to NGOs, including Human Rights First, by the USCIS Asylum Division on Dec. 16, 2009.

54 One Year Deadline Training, supra note 44 at 5.

55 "Clear and convincing" is described as "a firm belief or conviction as to the allegations sought to be established," though it does not need to be "conclusive or unequivocal." *Id* at 6-7.

56 *Id.* at 7-8.

57 *Id.* at 27-28. If the applicant was in another country less than a year before filing, his most recent entry into the United States must have been within the prior year to establish that he timely filed.

58 *Id.* at 6.This date is determined by the date/time stamp on the I-589 and in the asylum officer's RAPS system.

59 *Id.* at 6.

60 *Id.* at 8.

61 *Id.* at 9-12. Examples of changed circumstances are listed in the asylum regulations and Asylum Office training materials, though these lists are not exhaustive. 8 C.F.R. § 208.4(a)(4)(i).

62 *Id.* at 9.

63 *Id.* at 12-20. Examples of extraordinary circumstances are listed in the asylum regulations and Asylum Office training materials, though these lists are not exhaustive. 8 C.F.R. § 208.4(a)(5).

64 *Id.* at 13.

[65] *Id.* at 20-21. This standard of proof is lower than the "clear and convincing" standard; it is akin to "a preponderance of the evidence."

[66] *Id.* at 22. When determining reasonability, asylum officers should ask themselves "if a reasonable person under the same or similar circumstances as the applicant would have filed sooner." They should also "give applicants the benefit of the doubt."

[67] *Id.*

[68] Government Accountability Office, *U.S. Asylum System: Agencies Have Taken Actions to Help Ensure Quality in the Asylum Adjudication Process, but Challenges Remain,* GAO-08-935, 13 (Sept. 2008).

[69] *Supra* note 50.

[70] One Year Deadline Training, *supra* note 44.

[71] Information obtained from USCIS Asylum Division on June 16, 2009.

[72] HRF case 96234. Represented by *pro bono* counsel at Sidley Austin LLP through the Human Rights First Asylum Legal Representation Program.

[73] HRF case 96265. Represented by *pro bono* counsel at Greenberg Traurig LLP through the Human Rights First Asylum Legal Representation Program.

[74] *Executive Office for Immigration Review before the House Subcomm. On Immigration, Citizenship, Refugees, Border Security and International law of the House Comm. on the Judiciary,* 111th Cong. (2010) (statement of Karen T. Grisez, on behalf of the American Bar Association) *available at* http://judiciary.house.gov/hearings/pdf/Grisez100617.pdf

[75] *Supra* note 53.

[76] Philip G. Schrag, Andrew I. Schoenholtz, Jaya Ramji-Nogales, and James P. Dombach, "Rejecting Refugees: Homeland Security's Administration of the One-Year Bar to Asylum," DRAFT -- September 2010, *available at* http://papers.ssrn.com/sol3/papers.cfm?abstract_id+1684231###, at 2. Note the final version of the article will appear in the December 2010 issue of the William and Mary Law Review.

[77] As detailed in the HRF 2010 Pro Bono Survey, thirty-one of these cases were taken on by Human Rights First after they were rejected based on the filing deadline and referred into immigration court proceedings, and four of these cases were represented by HRF *pro bono* attorneys at the Asylum Office. Supra note 23.

[78] HRF 2010 Pro Bono Survey, *supra* note 23. Twenty-two of these applicants were granted asylum and four were granted or accepted withholding of removal.

[79] More information about Human Rights First filing deadline cases can be found in the Appendix.

[80] TRAC Immigration, Immigration Case Backlog Continues to Grow (Aug. 12, 2010), *available at* http://trac.syr.edu/immigration/reports/235/ (accessed September 17, 2010).

[81] TRAC Immigration, Backlog in Immigration Cases Continues to Climb (Mar. 11, 2010), available at http://trac.syr.edu/immigration/reports/225/ (accessed September 17, 2010).

[82] HRF case 95712. Represented by *pro bono* counsel at Fried, Frank, Harris, Shriver & Jacobson LLP through the Human Rights First Asylum Legal Representation Program.

[83] HRF case 95478. Represented by *pro bono* counsel at Gibson, Dunn & Crutcher LLP through the Human Rights First Asylum Legal Representation Program.

[84] HRF case 9568. Represented by *pro bono* counsel at White & Case LLP through the Human Rights First Asylum Legal Representation Program. The family's story was also profiled in **The New York Daily News**. Eric Herman, *Immigration: No Kid Glove,* NY Daily News, (Apr. 30, 2000); see also Jalloh statement, supra note 47.

[85] Human Rights First interview with Matt Sura, law student representative at University of Colorado Law School's Civil Practice Clinic (September 22, 2010).

[86] BIA Filing Deadline Case Analysis, *supra* note 22.

[87] *Supra* note 80.

[88] *See* Matter of Anon. (A# redacted) (BIA, Jan. 12, 2006) (on file with Human Rights First), obtained through Freedom of Information Act (FOIA) request filed by the National Immigrant Justice Center.

[89] *See* Matter of Anon. (A# redacted) (Jan. 16, 2008) (on file with Human Rights First), obtained through Freedom of Information Act (FOIA) request filed by the National Immigrant Justice Center.

[90] *See, e.g.,* American Bar Association Commission on Immigration: Reforming the Immigration System: Executive Summary (2010), *available at* http://new.abanet.org/Immigration/PublicDocuments/ReformingtheImmigrationSystemExecutiveSummary.pdf; TRAC Immigration, Immigration Courts: Still a Troubled Institution (June 30, 2009), available at http://trac.syr.edu/immigration/reports/210/ (accessed September 17, 2010); Appleseed, Assembly Line Injustice: Blueprint to Reform America's Immigration Courts 10-11 (May 2009), *available at* http://appleseeds.net/Portals/0/Documents/Publications/Assembly%20Line%20Injustice.pdf (accessed September 17, 2010).

[91] EOIR, FY 2009 Statistical Yearbook A 1-2 (Mar. 2010), available at http://www.justice.gov/eoir/statspub/fy09syb.pdf (accessed on September 17, 2010). See note 19 for asylum office statistical data. The overwhelming majority of cases rejected by the asylum office are referred into the immigration court removal process.

[92] EOIR does not keep statistics regarding the filing deadline, and the asylum office does not track the outcome of its filing deadline rejections at the immigration courts. However, as detailed in note 76 above, nearly 20,000 asylum cases would likely have been granted without immigration court litigation if not for the filing deadline.

[93] *Haniffa v. Gonzales,* 165 Fed. App'x 28, 29 (2d Cir. 2006).

[94] *Supra* note 30

[95] See Id.

[96] Human Rights First correspondence with Victoria Neilson, Esq., Legal Director, Immigration Equality, Feb. 22, 2010 and Aug. 16, 2010.

97   Human Rights First interview with Susan Benesch, Esq., former Fellow, Center for Applied Legal Studies, Georgetown University Law Center, (Washington D.C.), Nov. 18, 2009.

98   INA § 208(b)(3)(A); 8 C.F.R. § 208.21(a).

99   INA § 207(c)(2); 8 C.F.R. § 207.7.

100   Kate Jastram and Kathleen Newland, "Family Unity and Refugee Protection," in Refugee Protection in International Law: UNHCR's Global Consultations on International Protection, eds. Erika Feller, Volker Türk and Frances Nicholson (Cambridge: Cambridge University Press, 2003), pp555-603.

101   *See Haniffa v. Gonzales,* supra note 93.

102   *Id.*

103   *Mlambo v. Attorney General,* 297 Fed. App'x 198 (3d Cir. 2008) (unpublished).

104   *Ali v. Gonzales,* 231 Fed. App'x. 48 (2d Cir. 2007).

105   UNHCR Executive Committee, *Establishment of the Sub-committee and General, Conclusion No. 1 (XXVI),* ¶ f (1975); UNHCR Executive Committee, *Family Reunion, Conclusion No. 9 (XXVIII)* (1977); UNHCR Executive Committee, *Refugees Without an Asylum Country, Conclusion No. 15 (XXX),* ¶ e (1979); UNHCR Executive Committee, *Family Reunification, Conclusion No. 24 (XXXII)* (1981); UNHCR Executive Committee, *Refugee Children, Conclusion No. 47 (XXXVIII),* ¶ d (1987); UNHCR Executive Committee, *Conclusion on Refugee Children and Adolescents, Conclusion No. 84 (XLVIII),* ¶ b(i) (1997); UNHCR Executive Committee, *Conclusion on International Protection, Conclusion No. 85 (XLIX),* ¶¶ u-x (1998); UNHCR Executive Committee, *Conclusion on the Protection of the Refugee's Family, Conclusion No. 88 (L)* (1999); UNHCR Executive Committee, *Conclusion on Local Integration, Conclusion No. 104 (LVI),* ¶ n(iv) (2005).

106   International Covenant on Civil and Political Rights art. 23, Dec. 16, 1966, 999 U.N.T.S. 171. The United States ratified the ICCPR on June 8, 1992.

107   HRF cases 96587 and 96591. Represented by pro bono counsel at Patterson Belknap Webb & Tyler LLP through the Human Rights First Asylum Legal Representation Program.

108   HRF case 96390. Represented by *pro bono* counsel at Akin Gump Strauss Hauer & Feld LLP through the Human Rights First Asylum Legal Representation Program.

109   *INS Says Asylum Reform Efforts Are Working,* 72 No. 35 INTERPRETER RELEASES 1241, Sept. 11, 1995.

110   141 CONG. REC. E1635-01 (daily ed. Aug. 4, 1995) (statement of Rep. Franks).

111   For example, Sen. Alan K. Simpson (R-WY) explained about the deadline, "What you are seeing is, when you have a country that is your leading source of illegal immigration, they are picking them up, and they have been here 2, 3 years, and they say, 'I am seeking asylum' because they know that these procedures are interminable. That is what we are trying to get at. We are not after the person from Iraq, or the Kurd, or those people. We are after the people gimmicking the system." Rep. Charles Schumer (D-NY) was quoted as saying "If you believe enough in America to claim asylum, you ought to come forward and not wait till someone says, 'Gotcha.'" 142 CONG. REC. S4468 (daily ed. May 1, 1996) (statement of Sen. Simpson); *see also* Dugger, *supra* note 48.

112   142 CONG. REC. S11840 (daily ed. Sept. 30, 1996) (statement of Sen. Hatch).

113   "Let me say that I share the Senator's concern that we continue to ensure that asylum is available for those with legitimate claims of asylum. The way in which the time limit was rewritten in the conference report—with the two exceptions specified—was intended to provide adequate protections to those with legitimate claims of asylum. I expect that circumstances covered by the Senate's good cause exception will likely be covered by either the changed circumstances exception or the extraordinary circumstances exception contained in the conference report language." *Id.*

114   *INS Finalizes Asylum Reform Regulations,* 71 No. 46 INTERPRETER RELEASES 1577, Dec. 5, 1994.

115   *One Year Later: Asylum Claims Drop by 57 Percent,* 73 No. 2 INTERPRETER RELEASES, 46, Jan. 10, 1996. Prior to the reforms, INS had a two-track system for adjudicating asylum applications. Approximately 35% of applications were scheduled for an interview immediately and adjudication within 120-150 days. The other 65% were given no timetable for adjudication, instead joining the backlog. *INS Finalizes Asylum Reform Regulations,* 71 No. 46 INTERPRETER RELEASES 1578, Dec. 5, 1994.

116   Rules and Procedures for Adjudication of Applications for Asylum or Withholding of Deportation and for Employment Authorization, 59 Fed. Reg. 62,284 (1994) (to be codified at 8 C.F.R. pts. 208, 236, 242, 274a, and 299) ("The Department strongly believes that the asylum process must be separated from the employment authorization process. This rule will discourage applicants from filing meritless claims solely as a means to obtain employment authorization."). *See also* PISTONE, supra at note 11 at 7-8.

117   William Branigin, *Year-Long Campaign Slashes New Claims by 57%,* WASH. POST, Jan. 5, 1996, at A2.

118   *INS Says Asylum Reform Efforts Are Working,* 72 No. 35 INTERPRETER RELEASES 1241, Sept. 11, 1995.

119   This number does not include asylum applications filed as a result of the American Baptist Church settlement, which allowed Salvadorans and Guatemalans who had previously not been eligible for asylum to apply. *See* Branigin, "Year-Long Campaign Slashes New Claims by 57%," *supra* note 117.

120   Dugger, *supra* note 48.

121   Branigin, *supra* note 117. INS adjudicated 126,165 asylum cases in 1995, up from 60,788 in 1994.

122   *INS Announces Progress Five Years Into Asylum Reform,* 77 No. 6 INTERPRETER RELEASES 186-187, Feb. 7, 2000.

123   Walter Shapiro, "Human Faces Enforce Harsh Immigration Law," *USA Today,* April 10, 1998.

124   *INS Holds News Conference on the Asylum Reform Efforts,* FDCH POL. TRANSCRIPTS, Jan. 4, 1996.

125   *See supra.* Doris Meissner said the deadline would "seriously undercut [INS's] ability to maintain [the regulatory changes'] progress." Then Director of INS's Office of International Affairs Phyllis Coven asserted, "A deadline will gum up the process and have us spinning around an issue – when a person entered the country – which is difficult to prove, rather than just hearing the claim and getting to the substance." Dugger, *supra* note 48.

[126] Khandwala et al., *supra* note 12.

[127] Ilegal Immigration Reform and Immigrant Responsibility Act (IIRIRA), Pub. L. No. 104-208, Div. C, § 604(a), 110 Stat. 3009-690 (1996).

[128] Rules and Procedures for Adjudication of Applications for Asylum or Withholding of Deportation and for Employment Authorization, 59 Fed. Reg. 62284 (Dec. 5, 1994).

[129] INA § 208(d)(6).

[130] INA § 274C.

[131] Document and Benefit Fraud Task Force, U.S. Immigration and Customs Enforcement, *available at* http://www.ice.gov/partners/idbenfraud/idbenfraudtf.htm (accessed Dec. 18, 2009).

[132] *See* Careen Shannon, The Robert L. Levine Distinguished Lecture Overcoming Barriers to Immigrant Representation: Exploring Solutions: Report of Subcommittee 3: Addressing Inadequate Representation: Regulating Immigration Legal Service Providers: Inadequate Representation and Notario Fraud, 78 FORDHAM L. REV. 577, 591-599 (2009); Margaret Mikyung Lee, Cong. Res. Serv., Legal Ethics in Immigration Matters: Legal Representation and Unauthorized Practice of Law 13 (Sept. 18, 2009), *available at* http://www.abanet.org/publicserv/immigration/notario/crs_lega_ethics_in_immigration_matters.pdf.

[133] INA § 208(d)(5)(A).

[134] Affirmative Asylum Procedures Manual, U.S. Citizenship and Immigration Services 2-5 (2007), *available at* http://www.uscis.gov/files/nativedocuments/AffrmAsyManFNL.pdf [*hereinafter* Manual].

[135] *Id.* at 41.

[136] *Id.* at 12-13; Immigration Judge Bench Book, Executive Office for Immigration Review, *available at* http://www.justice.gov/eoir/vll/benchbook/tools/Script%20Initial%20Hearing.htm.

[137] *See supra* note 133.

[138] *See* Refugee Roulette, *supra* note 19 at 17 (citing correspondence with Joanna Ruppel, Deputy Dir., Asylum Div., U.S. Citizenship and Immigration Servs., U.S. Dep't of Homeland Sec.).

[139] *Supra* note 131 at 40.

[140] Forensic Document Laboratory, U.S. Immigration and Customs Enforcement, http://www.ice.gov/partners/investigations/services/forensiclab.htm (accessed Dec. 18, 2009).

[141] Press Release, American Immigration Lawyers Association, AILA Applauds Introduction of the "Immigration Fraud Prevention Act of 2009" (March 12, 2009), *available at* http://www.aila.org/content/default.aspx?docid=28256.

[142] G.M. Filisko, *Notoriety for Notarios: ABA project targets consultants who steer noncitizens afoul of U.S. immigration law*, ABA JOURNAL (Dec. 2009), *available at* http://www.abajournal.com/magazine/article/notoriety_for_notarios/.

[143] Fight Notario Fraud, ABA Commission on Immigration, http://new.abanet.org/Immigration/Pages/FightNotarioFraud.aspx (Accessed September 4, 2010).

[144] *See Matter of O-D-*, 21 I. & Dec. 1079 (BIA 1998) (denying asylum to an applicant who had submitted false documents in support of his claim and was found not to be credible).

[145] Human Rights First interview with "Dehab" (May 14, 2009). For reasons of confidentiality, the refugee's real name has not been used.

[146] INA § 208(a)(2)(D).

[147] 142 CONG. REC. S11839-40 (daily ed. Sept. 30, 1996) (statement of Sen. Hatch).

[148] 142 CONG. REC. S11840 (daily ed. Sept. 30, 1996) (statement of Sen. Hatch).

[149] 8 C.F.R. § 208.4(a)(4)-(5).

[150] 8 C.F.R. § 208.4(a)(4).

[151] 8 C.F.R. § 208.4(a)(5).

[152] 8 C.F.R. § 208.4(a)(4)(i), (5).

[153] Filing deadline data provided to NGOs, including Human Rights First, by the USCIS Asylum Division on Dec. 16, 2009. See note 19 regarding analysis of filing deadline statistics.

[154] Pistone & Schrag, *supra* note 10.

[155] *Id* at 16. See *e.g.*, Musalo & Rice, *supra* note 11. *See also* Corrected Brief of Human Rights First, the Center for Gender and Refugee Studies & the Harvard Immigration and Refugee Clinical Program et al. as Amici Curiae in Support of Petitioner, Gomis v. Holder, 175 L. Ed. 2d. 881 (2010), *available at* http://humanrightsfirst.org/asylum/probono/special/pb_special.aspx

[156] Stuart L. Lustig, *Symptoms of Trauma Among Political Asylum Applicants: Don't Be Fooled*, 31 HASTINGS INT'L & COMP. L. REV. 725, 725 (2008).

[157] *Id.* at 727.

[158] *Id.* at 726. See also Keller testimony, *supra* note 13.

[159] *HRF Report Women at Risk*, *supra* note 14 at 19 fn 7.

[160] *See* Mina Fazel, Jeremy Wheeler & John Danesh, *Prevalence of Serious Mental Disorder in 7000 Refugees Resettled in Western Countries: A Systemic Review*, 365 THE LANCET 1309 (2005) (reviewing 20 published surveys of refugees' mental health).

[161] 142 CONG. REC. S11840 (daily ed. Sept. 30, 1996) (statement of Sen. Hatch).

[162] 8 C.F.R. § 208.4(a)(5)(i).

[163] Lustig, *supra* note 156 at 731.

[164] *See Matter of Anon.* (A# redacted) (BIA, Jan. 12, 2006), *supra* note 88.

[165] Human Rights First interview on Oct. 30, 2008 with William Saupe, Esq.

[166] HRF case 96722. Represented by *pro bono* counsel at Mayer Brown LLP through the Human Rights First Asylum Legal Representation Program.

[167] See Musalo & Rice, *supra* note 11 at 704.

168 *See also* Matter of Anon. (A# redacted) (BIA, Jan. 25, 2006) (on file with Human Rights First). In this case, which was identified through a Freedom of Information Act production of BIA decisions, asylum was denied based on the filing deadline despite letters from physicians confirming the PTSD diagnosis. Despite several letters from physicians that confirmed a diagnosis of PTSD, the BIA held that "no evidence had been submitted that indicated how [the applicant's] medical problems prevented him from filing an asylum application."

169 *HRF Report Women at Risk, supra* note 14 at 14.

170 *Id.* at 16.

171 See Human Rights First, Renewing U.S. Commitment to Refugee Protection: Recommendations for Reform on the 30th Anniversary of the Refugee Act 17-18 (2010), available at http://www.humanrightsfirst.org/asylum/refugee-act-symposium/30th-AnnRep-3-12-10.pdf.

172 *See* Tahirih Justice Center, Precarious Protection: Unsettled Policy and Current Laws Harm Women and Girls Facing Persecution 35 (2009) http://www.tahirih.org/site/wp-content/uploads/2009/10/tahirihreport_precariousprotection.pdf.

173 *See* Victoria Neilson & Aaron Morris, *The Gay Bar: The Effect of the One-Year Filing Deadline on Lesbian, Gay, Bisexual, Transgender, and HIV-Positive Foreign Nationals Seeking Asylum or Withholding of Removal,* 8 N.Y. City L. Rev. 233, 263 (2005).

174 *Id.*

175 Medical Examination of Aliens – Removal of Human Immunodeficiency Virus (HIV) Inflection from Definition of Communicable Disease of Public Health Significance. 74 Fed. Reg. 56547 (Nov. 2, 2009) (to be codified at 42 C.F.R. pt. 34).

176 *HRF Report Women at Risk, supra* note 14 at 16; Nancy Kelly, *Gender-Related Persecution: Assessing the Asylum Claims of Women,* 26 Cornell Int'l L.J. 625, 626 (1993).

177 See Neilson & Morris, *supra* note 173 at 264.

178 See Musalo & Rice, *supra* note 11 at 705. This young woman eventually sought legal assistance from Human Rights First, and she is currently represented by *pro bono* attorneys at the firm of Reed Smith LLP through Human Rights First's Asylum Legal Representation Program.

179 Human Rights First interview with Prof. Phil Schrag, Director, Center for Applied Legal Studies, Georgetown University Law Center (Nov. 18, 2009). The man was represented by law students at the Center for Applied Legal Studies, Georgetown University Law Center.

180 HRF case 96501. Represented by *pro bono* counsel at Shearman & Sterling LLP through the Human Rights First Asylum Legal Representation Program.

181 Changed circumstances include "changes in conditions in the applicant's country of nationality." 8 C.F.R § 208.4(a)(4)(A).

182 Matter of Anon. (A# redacted) (BIA, Jan. 25, 2005) (on file with Human Rights First).

183 *See Al-Ghorbani v. Holder,* 585 F.3d 980 (6th Cir. 2009).

184 *Supra* note 103 at 200.

185 *See* Khandwala et al., *supra* note 12.

186 *See Soe v. Gonzales, supra* note 16. The petitioner's BIA brief is also on file with Human Rights First.

187 HRF case 89669. Represented by *pro bono* counsel at Paul, Weiss, Rifkind, Wharton & Garrison, LLP through the Human Rights First Asylum Legal Representation Program.

188 HRF case 96746. Represented by *pro bono* counsel at Fried, Frank, Harris, Shriver & Jacobson through the Human Rights First Asylum Legal Representation Program.

189 *See* Pistone & Schrag, *supra* note 10 at 25-26.

190 Andrew I. Schoenholtz & Jonathan Jacobs, *The State of Asylum Representation: Ideas for Change,* 16, Geo. Immigr. L. Rev. 739, 742 (2002); *see also* U.S. Government Accountability Office, *U.S. Asylum System: Significant Variation Existed in Asylum Outcomes across Immigration Courts and Judges,* 30, GAO-08-940 (Sept. 2008), http://www.gao.gov/new.items/d08940.pdf [*hereinafter* GAO, *U.S. Asylum System*].

191 TRAC: Asylum Denial Rate Reaches All Time Low: FY 2010 Results, a Twenty-Five Year Perspective, http://trac.syr.edu/immigration/reports/240/; *see also* GAO, *U.S. Asylum System,* supra note 190.

192 Refugee Roulette, *supra* note 19 at 287.

193 *Id.*

194 *See* Human Rights First, U.S. Detention of Asylum Seekers: Seeking Protection, Finding Prison 58-9 (2009), *available at* http://www.humanrightsfirst.org/pdf/090429-RP-hrf-asylum-detention-report.pdf.

195 *See* Pistone, *supra* note 12 at 7-8.

196 Human Rights First interview of May 7, 2009 with Regina Germain, Esq., former Legal Director, Rocky Mountain Survivors Center.

197 *See* Pistone & Schrag, *supra* note 10 at 27-28.

198 To make an ineffective assistance of counsel claim, an applicant must provide 1) an affidavit detailing the agreement between the applicant and the representative and how the representative did not meet his obligations; 2) proof that the representative has been informed about the ineffective assistance of counsel claim and given a chance to respond; 3) proof that the applicant has filed a complaint with the appropriate disciplinary authority. 8 C.F.R. § 208.4(a)(5)(iii); *Matter of Lozada,* 19 I. & N. Dec. 637 (BIA 1988).

199 Executive Office for Immigration Review, U.S. Department of Justice, Recognition and Accreditation Program, available at http://www.justice.gov/eoir/statspub/raroster.htm.

200 HRF case 72102. Represented by *pro bono* counsel at Milbank, Tweed, Hadley & McCloy LLP through the Human Rights First Asylum Legal Representation Program.

201 HRF case 96554. Represented by *pro bono* counsel at Skadden, Arps, Slate, Meagher & Flom LLP through the Human Rights First Asylum Legal Representation Program.

202 8 C.F.R. § 208.4(a)(4)(ii), (5).

203 Manual, *supra* note 134 at 22

204 *Id.*

[205] Human Rights First interview of May 7, 2009 with Regina Germain, Esq.

[206] Manual, *supra* note 134 at 24.

[207] HRF case 96343. Represented by *pro bono* counsel at Kaye Scholer LLP through the Human Rights First Asylum Legal Representation Program.

[208] *See Matter of Anon.* (A# redacted) (BIA, Jan. 31, 2007) (on file with Human Rights First).

[209] Human Rights First interview of Nov. 6, 2009 with Helen Harnett, Director of Policy, National Immigrant Justice Center.

[210] *See Martinez Ruiz v. Gonzales*, 479 F.3d 762 (11th Cir. 2007).

[211] *See Refugee Roulette, supra* note 19 at 77-88 (examining the rates of remands by circuit courts throughout the country); *see e.g. Gatimi v. Holder*, 578 F.3d 611, 615 (7ᵗʰ Cir. 2009) (vacating and remanding to the BIA based on BIA's failure to explain their reasoning in agreeing with the judge's decision to deny asylum based on female genital mutilation); *Baballah v. Ashcroft*, 367 F.3d 1067, 1076-77 (9ᵗʰ Cir. 2003) (finding that the judge ignored Baballah's numerous instances of mistreatment, which cumulatively amounted to persecution).

[212] INA § 208(a)(3); IIRIRA at § 604(a).

[213] INA § 242(a)(2)(D); REAL ID Act, Pub. L. No. 109-13, Div. B, § 106(a)(1)(A)(iii), 119 Stat. 310 (2005).

[214] For a detailed explanation on the circuit court split, see Petition for Writ of Certiorari at 20-26, Gomis v. Holder, 175 L. Ed. 2d. 881 (2010), available at http://www.aclu.org/files/assets/2009-8-11-GomisvHolder-CertPetition.pdf

[215] The Ninth Circuit has categorically held that "the application of law to undisputed facts" (otherwise called "mixed questions of law and fact") as presented in filing deadline claims is reviewable as a question of law under INA § 242(a)(2)(D). *Ramadan v. Gonzales*, 479 F.3d 646, 648 (9th Cir. 2007), *reh'g en banc denied* 504 F.3d 973 (9th Cir. 2007). The Second Circuit has similarly ruled that mixed questions of law and fact are reviewable, but cautions that it will "examine the precise arguments of the petition" to ensure that only legal questions are addressed. *Xiao Ji Chen v. U.S. Dep't of Justice*, 471 F.3d 315, 329-331 (2d Cir. 2006).

[216] BIA Filing Deadline Case Analysis, *supra* note 22.

[217] *See Zhu v. Gonzales*, 493 F.3d 588 (5th Cir. 2007).

[218] *Martinez Ruiz v. Gonzales*, 479 F.3d 762 (11th Cir. 2007), *supra* note 210.

[219] Taslimi v. Holder, 590 F.3d 981 (9th Cir. 2010). Additional details provided by the Immigration Judge's decision in the case (on file with Human Rights First).

[220] *See Ge v. Holder*, 588 F.3d 90 (2d Cir. 2009).